THE TORTOISE AND THE LYRE

AESTHETIC RECONSTRUCTIONS

Liberato Santoro-Brienza

IRISH ACADEMIC PRESS

Published by
IRISH ACADEMIC PRESS
Kill Lane, Blackrock, Co. Dublin, Ireland

and in the United States of America by

Irish Academic Press,
International Specialized Book Services
5804 NE Hassalo St.,
Portland, OR 97213.

A catalogue record for this title
is available from the British Library

ISBN 0-7165-2471-6

Printed and bound in Ireland
by Colour Books Ltd., Dublin

Contents

To mamma Vittoria, Mary, Louisa and Giuseppe

Foreword

"Beauty is the promise of happiness", wrote Stendhal. Liberato Santoro-Brienza's book on aesthetics, *The Tortoise and the Lyre,* explores many of the promises made by Western works of art, from the earliest origins of Greek civilisation to current movements in European literature and cinema. He brings his many years of experience as a university lecturer in philosophy and aesthetics to bear on a rich and varied terrain.

Beginning with the intriguing story of Hermes, child-god of techne, art and craft, the author clarifies the deep insights of Greek mythology into the process of artistic creativity. It was Hermes, we are reminded, the *enfant terrible* of the Olympian world, who leapt from his mother's heavenly womb in search of the secrets of invention. The fruits of his mischievous discoveries are recorded for us in the anonymous *Hymn to Hermes,* dating back almost three thousand years, which celebrates the birth of art in the tale of *The Tortoise and the Lyre*, from which this book takes its felicitous title.

Taking his cue from this legendary tale, the writer proceeds in his first five chapters to examine definitions of art and tragedy in the poetics of Aristotle, the first great philosopher of aesthetics. From there, we are lead along a fascinating path of investigation through the aesthetic theories of Neo-Platonism, which so profoundly informed Medieval thought, to those of Hegel who inaugurated the modern discussion of poetics with his apocalyptic announcement of the death of art. Subsequent chapters extend the field of enquiry to include original studies on Adorno, structuralism, the avant-garde, and semiotics.

The second section of the book, entitled "Critical Explorations", follows the author on a return journey to the poetic riches of his native Italian culture. The studies here range from Dante's *Paradiso* to the cinematic masterpieces of Fellini and Olmi, and finally to the novelistic *tour de force* of Eco's *The Name of the Rose*. It is gratifying to witness this fitting tribute being paid by the author to the aesthetic work of Umberto Eco, his mentor and compatriot.

In his conclusion, the author makes a plea for the forging of new aesthetic paths to reconstruction. This is indeed a valuable reminder in our age of baleful pessimism, when prophets of extremity hold sway in so many debates on the end of art, that there is still an indispensable place for reconsidering the enduring triad of artistic virtues: beauty, creativity, and transcendence. I am sure that the readers of this volume will take as much pleasure in reading it as the author so patently has taken in writing it.

Professor Richard Kearney
Department of Philosophy,
University College, Dublin.

Preface

This book is an invitation and an introduction to some of the main themes, problems and questions in the field of aesthetics and poetics. The topics presented and discussed can be read as self-sufficient and self-contained, no matter how open-ended, explorations. The author would hope, at once, that the individual chapters may so interact as to contribute towards a mapping, no matter how asymptotic, of the central areas of art and of philosophy.

The main idea that guides the discourse articulated in these pages is that art must be understood as a privileged space of ever increasing creativity. The model and inspiration of semiotic enquiry have assisted, by reminding us that *all is a sign* to be patiently, carefully, generously decoded and interpreted. Hence the need to revisit venerable philosophical themes and theses. Hence the attention to the speculative resources to be found in past thinkers. Hence also the continuous reference to texts, and the philological, hermeneutical excavations, to let arguments emerge from their own theoretical and cultural contexts.

The obvious and all-pervasive presence of semiotic discourse, especially echoing the voice of Umberto Eco, reinforces and warrants the reconstructive intentions of this book. In an implicit manner, this book is a statement about order, in whatever form it may come to light. It may also prove to be the instance of an alternative to and a witness against the abuses of extreme deconstructive tenets.

I hasten to add that, far from presuming completeness, this book hopes only to be a useful guide. It has been written primarily with paedagogical intentions, for students of the discipline. I shall be gratified if it will prove its worth as a companion introduction to the field of philosophy and aesthetics. I shall be more gratified if it will meet with some degree of approval from colleagues and specialist scholars.

In a way, this volume is the result of past teaching. I owe most of it to my students. In a way, I am repaying an old debt. Some of the material presented here had been published, in the form of essays and papers, in various philosophical and academic journals. I have retrieved some of those earlier publications because they seemed to present and articulate ideas now as pertinent and relevant, as when I discussed them for the first time. If a further justification were needed, I would gladly borrow Pascal's thought: "Qu'on ne dise pas que je n'ai rien dit de nouveau: la disposition des matieres est nouvelle".

I have many to thank for the inception and the completion of this work: past students, colleagues, family and friends. Particular thanks to Prof. Richard Kearney for his generous *foreward* and his sensitive acknowledgement. My sincere thanks to Dr Fergus D'Arcy, Dean of the Arts Faculty, and to Prof. Dermot Moran for their support and encouragement. Quite particularly, I must give my thanks to Mr Mark Dooley, one of our outstanding post-graduates, who has assisted, with undivided attention, admirable enthusiasm and remarkable energy, in preparing, editing, computing, formatting the script. More so, he has acted as counsel and adviser, on numerous occasions. The best way in which I could possibly express my gratitude to Mark is by wishing him the fruitful and distinguished future which he doubtlessly deserves and which he surely will realise. I must finally confess my affectionate gratitude to Mary, my wife, and to Louisa and Peppe, my children. Their caring love has been continuous and reliable sustenance in my academic as well as existential journey. They are inexhaustible sources of much happiness and serenity. They inspire a sense of order without which no nourishing thought could take form and utterance.

Hermes and the Semiotics of Art

What is beauty? It is not light and it is not night, perhaps a twilight, the birth of truth and of un-truth, something in-between. (Goethe)

Too late for the gods, as Heidegger put it, and too late for the a-problematic conception of artistic beauty as epiphany of a world-order, we have been for long separated from the classical world where myths of artistic creativity abound.

Hermes, Orpheus, Daedalus, come readily to mind. Of these mythical protagonists, all carriers of deep intuitions and pertinent messages, I have always found Hermes the most fascinating and the most eloquent. The story of Hermes articulates a series of uncanningly contemporaneous insights, enlightening and relevant to our own understanding of art.

The anonymous *Hymn to Hermes,* presumably of the Eight or Seventh century B.C., celebrates, among other attributes of the god, the birth of art and announces some essential traits of artistic production and creativity. The hymn sings of Hermes and of his mother, *the shy goddess, the rich-tressed, curley-haired Maia.* Hermes is conceived in a deep, shady cave where Zeus came secretly, *unseen by deathless gods and mortal men,* to love the beautiful nymph. Conceived in secrecy, *in the deep darkness of night,* Hermes is also secretly born *at dead of night.*

From the very beginning we understand this god to be of quite uncommon disposition. Indeed, son of Maia the midwife, Hermes is not begotten after common lengthy labour. As the god of *techne,* art and craft, production and forth-bringing, *Hermes leaped from his mother's heavenly womb.* We see this child-god projected, at his very birth, towards the world, matter and nature; restlessly eager to attend to his appointed task. The ingenuity, the creativity, the curiosity, the metamorphic powers of the god leave him no time to waste. *So soon had he leaped from his mother's heavenly womb, he lay not waiting in his holy cradle, but he sprang up and sought the oxen of Apollo. The infant*

1

terrible of the Olympian world entertains mischievous thoughts on how to steal some of his brother's sacred cattle. His inexhaustible appetite for adventure and crafty deeds is aptly suggested by his craving for a prime roast! Hermes seeks and finds the sacred herd; puts to sleep the hundred eyes of the giant Argos, guardian of Apollo's oxen; wears on his baby feet a huge bundle of reeds, to frustrate detection; walks backwards, pulling six cattle by their tail, to contrive a cunning alibi that may allow him to disown his deed...The god of art and craft, who *grasped the art of fire, the original skill of producing fire from sticks* (for the purpose of roasting the stolen beef!), is also a thieving, deceitful, crafty god. Even in this, Hermes is quite convincing and exceedingly endearing.

The myth of Hermes, as recorded in the hymn, is rich and varied, packed with insight, quite inspiring. It is a polyhedric narrative of a polysemic message. In particular, however, it grants us access to the original understanding of art, of its beginning and of its essential features. Ready to test his cunning and anxious to exercise his powers of production, invention and transformation, Hermes abandons the comfort of his cradle. *But as he stepped over the threshold of the high-roofed cave, he found a tortoise there and gained endless delight.* On the threshold of that mythical cave, as on the threshold or the in-between of presence and absence, an interface, we witness the birth of art, the alchemy of artistic creation, the structure of artistic processes.

Hail, lovely in shape, comrade at the feast, sounding at the dance, well pleasing at sight from afar, good dancer, beautiful toy ! With these, and such-like attributes, the terrible god addresses the timid defenceless creature. With his flattering deceit, Hermes convinces the suspicious creature that it would be safer to go and live indoors. He adds:

> Living you shall be a spell against mischievous witchcraft [for the tortoise's flesh was reputedly endowed with magical powers, as Pliny reminds us]. But, the god proceeds, if you die, then you shall make sweetest song.

The tortoise is charmed, reassured, convinced by the flattering attributes that flourish and abound in the god's address. The creature trusts the god, allowing him to get closer, unable to decode the god's diction. The threshold is there, awaiting also the tortoise and, with it, the whole of nature. For, not literally but only by implication and abduction, only by metaphoric figuration and formal transformation, only

by metaphoric intentionality, only by creative decodification and interpretation Hermes speaks of the mountain tortoise.

> Thus speaking he took up the tortoise, his charming toy. And as a swift thought
> darts through the heart of a man when thronging cares haunt him, or as bright
> glances flash from the eye, so glorious Hermes planned both thought and deed
> at once.

He catches the creature, *cuts off its limbs and scoops out the marrow of
the mountain tortoise with a scoop of grey iron.* With the aid of reeds
and strings, the god makes finally the lyre. Now we understand the full
meaning of the god's *endless delight* engendered by the intentionally an-
ticipated act of creative transformation.

Now it is also clear what the poem means when it announces that *it
was Hermes who first made the tortoise a singer.* The wealth of this insight which I will presently translate into the language of contemporary
aesthetics, can be more fully appreciated if we briefly consider some of
the other distinguished attributes of Hermes announced in the hymn.
Insofar as he excels in giving convincing reasons, even when lying; insofar as he knows how to avail of the apt word for the achievement of
his own, sometimes crafty and sly, aims, Hermes finally becomes the
god of speech and the patron of eloquence. In virtue of this ability,
Hermes is also the herald and messenger of the gods: hence the intermediary interpreter and translator between the gods and the humans.
Furthermore, Hermes symbolises the experience of mediation, and
therefore the threshold, as the guide of the human souls in their journey
towards the light of life and, at once, towards the dark underworld of
death. The nocturnal side of his character makes him the god protector
of thieves, travellers and adventurers.

As skillful, crafty producer of metamorphoses and as messenger,
guide, interpreter and mediator, Hermes is the intermediary. *It was
Hermes who first made the tortoise a singer.* Hermes symbolises the
experience of artistic production as the process of transformation of
nature into culture, instanced in the transformation of nature into
culture, of the tortoise into the musical instrument and, hence, into
music itself. However, the process of transformation and production,
which art is, presupposes or at least implies another kind of process and
another kind of experience, of which art itself is but one instance. I
mean the discovery of language and the "linguistic constitution of the
human world" as culture or codified experience. At the sight of the

tortoise, Hermes *gains endless delight*. He laughs, for he sees the humble creature and something else: the lyre. More precisely, in order to transform the tortoise, the god sees it *as* something else. He sees nature as culture. He symbolises the fundamental and primordial event which characterises the very birth of humanity: the irruption of sign processes in the world of nature, the invention of signs. The myth of Hermes suggests that in order to transform the tortoise into the lyre and song, the god must have first seen the creature as *standing for* something else. He must have understood the tortoise as *the sign* of something else.

This points us in the direction of a semiotic foundation of all human experience and culture and, particularly, of the semiotic foundation of art processes. It points us to the semiotic character of works of art.

In the universe of human culture we can consider, with some profit, the work of art as a sign or message. Art stands as a distinguishing feature of the human world, just as language and sign-processes are the pertinent trait of human experience. We could even say that humanity came into being with the beginning of sign-processes and the invention of sign-function. The human mind, with its ability to inform and transform nature, was born when the first humans *saw something as something else:* a stone as a flint, a cave as a shelter, a branch as a weapon, a fur as the clothing, a sound/word as a concept...

Captives to the inner dynamism of that truly revolutionary quality-leap, we build our world as an endless process of signification. Works of art, far from escaping the realm of semiosis, constitute privileged occurrences of signification. They instance, more acutely than any other type of signs, the character of human existence as *in-between,* interface, inter-space, narrative and *threshold.* For, if works of art are signs and messages, they are nonetheless quite clearly distinguished from all other signs in the universal economy of language and of human production of artefacts. Works of art are characterised, and hence separated from other signs, as primarily *self-referential, polysemic and ambiguous* signs/messages. Unlike other artefacts, such as tools and implements, primarily intentionalised to their particular use or function, and hence primarily *pointing to* their pragmatic application; works of art point to themselves as instances of self-sufficient and self-inclusive form. As self-referential, the aesthetic sign/message/text points to itself, is viewed, perceived, contemplated primarily for its own sake: it attracts to its very presence, its structure, its form. Upon this are grounded the work's claim to autonomy and uniqueness, and our experience of the work as a self-inclusive, organic totality. The work's claim to aesthetic autonomy invites us, and, indeed, compels us, to focus upon its individual structure, hence prompting us to an ever-renewed act of reading. To put it otherwise, the self-focussing character of aesthetic messages, that gratify and stimulate, hence expand, our perception and our experience, is triggered, warranted and sustained by its unfamiliar, estranging, somewhat gratuitous, improbable, ambiguous and polysemic structure. Works of art are instances of novelty: they are fragments, vectors and vehicles of unprecedented sensibility; ever new attempts at re-ordering and re-constructing our experience of the world; ever renewed questions and answers to the enigma of our existence as threshold: in-between time and eternity, presence and absence, life and death, silence and utterance, joy and sadness.

The strangeness and ambiguity of aesthetic works, and hence the unavoidable *difficulty* we experience in *reading* them, stems from the challenge which every work of art addresses to previous conventions and codes. Though rooted in their own tradition, though unavoidably contextualised, works of art are what they are, and do what they do, or they affect us as they do, because they intentionally violate, at least in some respect, the pre-existing rules, codes and conventions. They certainly challenge and violate our everyday prosaic way of perceiving/experiencing the world. But insofar as works of art violate the norm and challenge previous codifications, structures and grammars, they constitute themselves as messages that claim, at once, the characters of individual languages or new codes. The poetics of modern art, particularly since its avant-garde inception, operates according to the mentioned semiotic strategy. For this reason, it can be rightly called a poetics of experimentation. Hence, again, the need for a patient and focussed attention, in our reading. Hence the demands and difficulty of sensitive response. Hence, finally, the enrichment and expansion of sensibility, the experience of delight and gratification, that every work of art affords us.

The classical world, the pre-modern world, signified by symbols of integration, could innocently rely on the desire for a closed order of things. Even those worlds, however, suspected the disruptive power or at least the challenge of art. The myth of Hermes, articulated in the Pseudo-Homeric hymn, playfully records that experience of violation as transformation and ritual sacrifice which art aims at reproducing. Challenge, disruption, transformation, *metamorphosis into form,* are inbuilt in the very essence of art as open-ended semiosis and as in-between. Art and its open works tell us the story of human experience as threshold: not a boundary, but an open space of the soul where change, transition, transformation, freedom, meaning, and growth of meaning take place.

Perhaps in this precisely lies the vocation of art: in finding new openings, new clearings, new margins and new thresholds. Perhaps Borges was thinking of this when he wrote:

> Music, moments of happiness, mythology, faces fatigued by time, some twilights and some places strive to tell us something, perhaps did utter some meaning that we should not have forgotten, or perhaps are on the point of telling us something: the imminence of a revelation that never quite occurs is perhaps what we call the aesthetic fact.

Towards a Definition of Art

A spider performs operations that resemble those of a weaver and a bee, in the construction of its wax cells, puts to shame human architects. However, that which, to begin, distinguishes the worst architect from the most skilled bee is that he has constructed the cell in his head before realising it in the wax. (K. Marx)

Art is a *practical modality,* a mode of action, a manner of making: an open field of forces, the horizon of the human experience of formation, in-formation and ordering objective, external reality. Art is, generally, a way and a manner of bridging the interval between spirit and matter, the soul and the world, the rational/intelligible and the sensuous/sense-perceptible. Art is a mode and a horizon of human encounters with a previously alien reality, *the earth,* which, thanks to the order-giving and informing power of art, is brought inward, is subjectivised and spiritualised, thus becoming a *world.* In art and through art man encounters nature and transforms it into culture. Consequently, art is an existential modality which specifies man's existence as such.

The artistic informative making which is intentional, that is teleologically conceived and exercised, and conscious of the art-ness or artificiality of the artistic manner of making, presupposes thought and knowledge.[1] Insofar as it is a particular modality of experience, as the human manner of actively and formatively encountering the outer realm of nature and matter, art concretely occurs and is given according to many *categorial* modes.[2]

The manner of making according to art, which is a conscious operation and a *knowing-how-to-do,* presupposes a categorial consciousness, a way of addressing oneself to:

1. what is not yet formed, the materials;
2. what is foreseen as the result of the formative act;
3. what is chosen as the forming principle or form;
4. what gives form, the human agent, the artist who avails of his/her own category of man-as-artist understood, indeed self-understood, even before and then during and after the ordering and informing

act/process. Diverse manners of making-doing according to art are given, subsequent to the categorial conception that one holds of oneself, of one"s organs of dialogue, formation and communication; of the outer reality and its potential disposition to fulfil a particular goal and achieve a particular result. This means that every manner of making-doing according to art, every model of art-making and every act of art-making is guided by a fundamental category or system of categories:

1. a conception of the materials, and of matter as such;
2. a conception of the goals at the fulfilment of which the made "thing", the artefact, aims, and of goal or purpose as such;
3. a conception of the making and of the principles which govern the same activity of making;
4. a conception of man-as-artist and of humanity in general.

Every form and experience of art presupposes a categorial concept of truth, no matter how implicit, inarticulate and unexpressed it may be. This is so if we understand truth as the adequate and making-adequate, adequating, encounter of mind, the forming and order-giving mind, in this case, and of the reality of nature and matter; furthermore, every act of making presupposes, and at once crystallises and constitutes a categorial conception of man and the world. It presupposes a vision and a revelation of reality in its totality, which is precisely what we mean by *truth*. Truth is reality, as such, brought to the light of consciousness.

What has been said could be briefly reformulated as follows: truth is the encounter of opposites, the synthesis, unity. There are as many conceptions of synthesis and unity (which is finally order and ordering, form and forming) as there are conceptions of truth.

We are accustomed to read and hear that art is a child of its time. The *time*, or times, is the culture, the ambient complex of ideas, facts, events, occurrences and experiences. The *time* is time of humanity, human time, civilisation, epoch and world in totality: with its God and its gods; with its myths, idols and fetishes; with its human inhabitants, with nature and infra-human things; with the ideas, the images and the human projects which aim at creating the conditions in which "the calamities will cease on earth", to echo Plato's ideal and aspiration. Every form of art, at different times, presupposes its world and a knowledge, no matter how weak and confused, of this world. It presupposes a sense of the world, even though such a sense may not be a clear and distinct idea, but may rather dwell in the pre-conscious and motivate human thought and actions, as a universal presupposition and epochal presupposition: as an ideal pre-knowledge.[3] Art presupposes a conception of truth. We are not thinking here of scientific and philosophic conceptual models. We would rather suggest that art-experiences presuppose and embody an intuitive grasp of the wordly state of affairs and, at once, inspire and suggest a new grasp of reality and, consequently, new dimensions of a renewed constitution of the world.

The theory of art, *qua* philosophical theory, explores the experience and essence of art in the diverse manifestations ordained by substrate epochal categories, interpreting them as concrete illuminations of these categories. The theory of art, aesthetics in its broadest sense, should aim primarily at elucidating the necessary relationship which obtains between every modality of making in art and the categories, the epochal categories and the truth of the world.

1. In its widest, most comprehensive and most general sense, *art* is the horizon of the human experience of transformation of the world, nature, things, materials, external reality, in order to produce *artefacts* [4]

2. *Fine art* is the horizon of the human experience of order-giving, transformation, information and formation of the world, nature, things, materials, external reality, in order to produce aesthetically *beautiful* artefacts.

1.i Nature does not produce artefacts. It does not produce things outside of itself and from outside. Nests and dens, of insects, fishes, birds and terrestrial animals are but apparently artefacts. In truth they are necessary extensions, indeed *organs* of nature. They are, necessarily and deterministically, organs of the process of self-preservation and self-realisation of nature in its species and individuals.

It would perhaps be worth illustrating this point, thus announcing its complexity and its problematic implications. We can initially say that there are no bees without bee-hives. etc. There are on the contrary humans, there is humanity, it would seem, without...shoes and without artefacts in general. The artefact, in the very general sense of the word, and in its pre-artistic meaning, is *produced from outside* and remains, in itself, an accidental event. The artefact does not constitute, intrinsically and exhaustively, the humanity of the humans. The artefacts, produced by the human hands, are not *organs* but *accidental extensions* of our hands. One could, at this stage, foresee the justifiable objection to be raised from a Marxian point of view, according to which man is truly man in consequence of his self-production through labour, i.e. through the production of artefacts. May it suffice here to indicate (and this may not represent an exhaustive answer to the problem) that:

a) it would be anti-humanitarian, and therefore opposed to the best aspirations of Marxism viewed in its philosophical and humanitarian light, to affirm that, for instance, John *is* a shoemaker, meaning that the total reality, the total existence and the total dignity of John is exhausted in and adequately represented by John's acts aimed at producing artefacts-shoes;

b) it would, on the other hand be much more correct and indeed more just to recognise that the work exercised in view of the production of artefacts, is finally exercised in view of the fulfilment of higher goals, higher than the shoes..., such as, for instance, leisure and the exercise of free, imaginative and spiritual activities. Spiritual activities, insofar as spiritual, do not aim at the production of artefacts, at least of pre-artistic artefacts.

With reference to the question of the possibility that nature may produce artefacts, let us finally say that nature does not *make* objects outside of itself and, furthermore, does not make *according to art,* but rather operates according to deterministic laws and inner necessity. Totally deprived of freedom, nature grows out of itself towards its self-preservation.

1.ii In some cases, nature (e.g. the domestic cat and the decorative indoor plants) utilises some artefacts, it finalises them to its own purpose, one could say. The domestic cat drinks and eats from the bowl, and sleeps on beds, carpets and armchairs. The cat uses the bowl precisely as a bowl, and the armchair precisely as an armchair. Armchairs are tools made for the purpose of resting on them, and bowls are tools made for containing food of a sort. Of the delicate indoor plants one knows how they would perish if exposed to the rigours of outdoor climatic conditions. The domestic, indoor plant aids its growth-process by means of the artefact house.

2.i Nature does not produce beautiful artefacts. But it can appear to be beautiful to the eye of beholding humans. We speak of a beautiful landscape, a beautiful flower, a beautiful cat, etc. It is quite clear, on the one hand, that nature exhibits such qualities and characters as: organic growth, finality, dynamic and vital order of a sort. And such-like characters and qualities we recognise in and attribute to beautiful art-works. It is no less clear, on the other hand, that a serene moonlit night may perhaps enchant and fill with wonder, may indeed be beautiful for young people in love. Quite certainly, though, the very same night, at the same time, would seem to be cold and cruel to the solitary wanderer overwhelmed and saddened by a sudden calamity. It would be far from easy to harmonise and to establish an agreement among all possible opinions, because it would be impossible to establish an agreement among all the possible, most diversified and individual states of mind which underlie the opinative appreciation of natural phenomena and their so-called beautiful aspects.

2.ii In no case whatsoever nature (cats, plants, bees) receives and enjoys the aesthetic artefact as beautiful/aesthetic. In some cases, perhaps in most if not even in all cases, nature perceives the sensible aspects of the beautiful artefact much more clearly than humans do. "Unlike bees we cannot see ultraviolet. Our sharpness of vision cannot match that of a hawk, to whom a miniature would seem merely impressionist".[5] Nature may hear more harmonics of a symphony, may see more colours of a painting, may appreciate more precisely than humans do the distances and measures of an architectural space, etc. Nature, nonetheless, fails to grasp the *art* of the artefact. It fails to grasp the beauty of a beautiful art-work. It does not and cannot grasp the *ergon*. Because the *ergon* is the life and the form, the act and the activity, the spirit, the language and the content of the artwork and of the soul whence it proceeds.

3. The beautiful is that which pleases, not because useful or in any way subordinate and intrinsically dependent upon other criteria and upon intrinsic goals and functions, but because in itself pleasing. The finest ancient oriental bowl, of high quality, pleases the thorough-bred pedigree cat of the millionaire Roman lady, because of the cream and the liver-pate which it contains! The Eighteenth century flower gardens of Rome may please bees and butterflies, for the pollen, the scents and

the colours produced by the growing vegetation. The same gardens pleased Goethe, for quite different reasons, one should hope! And precisely the difference of those reasons is the reason for the difference between Goethe and the bees.

Insofar as pleasing, the beautiful is beautiful in itself and, at once, for us. The pleasing pleases someone, it is pleasing for someone. The objective-subjective beautiful pleases in a universal manner, because it pleases *freely*, without ulterior motives. Insofar as freely pleasing, the beautiful pleases in a spiritual manner, intelligently, according to intellect and reason. It pleases truly, i.e. it pleases in a significant and meaningful way.

3.i The beautiful cannot be reduced to the functional. It has, insofar as beautiful, no purpose *outside of itself*. The beautiful means always more than its usage may indicate. But here a problem arises with reference to at least some beautiful artefacts. Let us think, for instance, of artistic architectural works. It is quite clear that buildings, even the architecturally most significant and most artistically designed, do not just stand there to be looked at. Clearly, in other words, architectural buildings cannot be evaluated in abstraction from their function and functionality. It is equally clear nonetheless that, although the efficient functionality of an edifice is an essential requirement and quality of the architectural work, the utility-function is sublimated and celebrated in the artistically significant and beautiful architectural artefact, precisely in its artistic form. The particular building may not necessarily be endowed with artistically beautiful form, in which case it would simply fail to be artistically significant, while, on the other hand, proving exceptionally well adequate to the foreseen functional purposes and for the fulfilment of these purposes. In other words, the beauty of the architectural work *adds* to the work a quality which will render the artefact pleasing in itself, somewhat independently of the utilisation of the object in question. It would seem, therefore, that also the architecturally beautiful work, which must be useful, means more than its function and usage. Furthermore, and insofar as what has just been said could well be applicable to any artefact, we would remark that the beautiful artefact intentionally manifests a *residuate* which escapes and defies any criterion of evaluation other than that of functionally indeterminate pleasingness. Consequently, the beautiful is use-less, it has no exchange-value, it is not a commercial good. Therefore it does not obey any law of supply and demand. It is not quantifiable, it is not reproducible, it can neither be copied nor translated: not in its being precisely what it is, not in its being beautiful.

The beautiful is, in one word, unique. In a deep and mysterious sense, it is a sacral event, a somewhat inscrutable qualitative occurrence, a moment of simple creativity, a totalising rite, a ritual celebration of reality. And this because the beautiful is *complete,* an organic totality finalised in itself. It is a value and a goal. The self-finalised is the organic. The organic is the dynamic totality, the total process of organs and organism, of parts and whole. It is life itself: the game, the players and the moves. It is the synthesis of spirit and matter: love, knowledge and body.

3.ii First and foremost, the beautiful artefact pleases in itself, without ulterior motives and free of prior determinations. It stands as an *absolutum*: absolved, purged of extrinsic links and ties. Contrariwise, the beautiful bowl is a bowl nonetheless, a tool. It is a tool that pleases. (Perhaps the difference between the artistically significant architectural work and the tool-bowl could be expressed as follows: the successfully artistic architectural work is *beautiful* while being useful and functional, the finely shaped and decorated bowl is *useful* while being beautiful).[6]
A bowl, furthermore, while pleasing some and displeasing others, although subject to the determinations of individual taste, can be understood, thought of, evaluated, acquired and used by *all* people, no matter how different their taste!, precisely *as* a bowl. Think of how many bowls we purchase, though finding them not particularly pleasing or even not pleasing at all! We finally get accustomed to their appearance, also thanks to the fact that we concentrate upon and acquire the habitual regard of their properties and functional qualities, according to which we habitually utilise and categorise them. On the other hand, how many Greek and Japanese bowls and vases have ceased to be bowls and vases in the museums and art-galleries of the world!
It does not seem that the same analysis could be applied to architectural art-work. If we were to commission the edification or the construction of an architecturally, artistically significant, i.e. beautiful *villa,* we would certainly demand and expect that the place of our future habitation, the commissioned dwelling-place, be a useful and functional arte-

fact, but furthermore that it be, first and foremost, a beautiful and pleasing dwelling place. We would certainly refuse to be presented with a merely functional, totally unattractive and stereotyped dwelling place. And, indeed, the villas designed by Le Corbusier or by Frank Lloyd Wright are at once useful, functional and extremely significant i.e. beautifully and pleasingly celebrative of that human experience which we call dwelling, home, living space. The way in which the masterpieces are functional does not differ in any significant way from the humble and modest, but functional, house purchased with knowledge of the criteria of functionality. There the functional aspects may simply be overemphasised and generously over-developed; they would, nonetheless, basically fail to determine the criterion of differentiation between themselves, villas by Le Corbusier, and other dwelling places, the house of judicious and practical citizens. The only significant and essential difference between the villas designed by Le Corbusier or Wright and the standard type of suburban house consists precisely in this: that the former are formally significant, i.e. beautiful. They are, first and foremost, pleasing etc. The analysis which we have outlined with reference to the beautiful architectural work would not seem to apply to what we may now call primarily useful artefacts. If one were to ask Picasso for a set of artistically designed bowls, the commissioner or client should not at all be surprised if he were to be presented, by the hands of the master, with bottomless bowls. He should, on the other hand, be extremely deluded and surprised if the Picassian bowls were adequately useful, while resembling the most conventional, stereotyped, industrially produced objects.

We may finally say that the beautiful and the functional constitute and invoke different parameters of evaluation, because they are in themselves constituted by different modes of intentionality. In the case of the the beautiful artefact an organic, intrinsically and immanent goal is expressly manifested and indeed principally constitutive of its pleasing beauty. In the case of the useful artefact, we see it constituted as for something else, therefore according to an instrumental, accidental, extrinsic and *transient goal*.

The beautiful and the useful are two different intentionalities which reduce and manifest the world of human artefacts. Intentionally we are primarily concerned with the pure presence of the aesthetic artefacts. They are *primarily* for-themselves, primarily signs of themselves.

Intentionally we are concerned with the functional employment of useful artefacts: they are *primarily* for something else, primarily signs of something else.

4. The pleasing of the beautiful, insofar as it is organic, immanent, absolute and totalised in itself, must be universal, for it is subjective as much as objective. This is to say that the pleasure/pleasing of the beautiful must be and is experienced by the subject as subject, and not by this or that empirical subject totally and exclusively immersed in his solitary and contingent finitude. The individual, empirical subject is limited by his particular degree of taste or education, his personal prejudices and opinions, his particular physical and mental disposition, his private interests and desires, his passions and emotions or lack of passions and emotions, his deficiencies, his social, cultural, historical determinations.

4.i In other words, the pleasure/pleasing of the beautiful is experienced by humans in their humanity, according to their being humans. It is experienced as an authentic human activity and, furthermore, it actually constitutes and determines the humanity of humans. We recognise the mark of humanity in the art-works of the past, much more than in the historical events and the recounted records of the same in the annals of historiographies.[7]

4.ii The pleasing of the beautiful is an anthropological experience: physical and spiritual unitedly. It is a synthetic, unifying, harmonic and self-finalised experience. If this is true, this experience is such that in it and through it the empirically determined individual human transcends himself towards himself. In art man overcomes his solitary finitude and celebrates the liberating experience of an unending dialogue. The experience of the beautiful reveals man's nature: his being on the borderline between time and eternity. In art man experiences his creative power of overcoming, always anew, the realm of the already given and of transforming his same given condition into ever new projects of himself and of the world.

5. The beautiful artefact is a linguistic-semantic event. As such it is structured and produced as a chain and process of communication. For

the artefact to be produced, the following elements, links of the chain (and dialectical *moments*) must be given: the artist; the means, tools and materials; the idea of the work, the significant and signified content or message; the form, the signifier; the receiver, the interpreter, the beholding observer, listener and spectator. In the art-work and in art, we could say, the world in totality is revealed as a system of signs, as a linguistic and communicative system in totality. Art is the process of manifestation of the linguistic constitution of the world.

5.i With remarkable obstinacy a large number of historians, critics and philosophers of art conventionally apply, particularly with reference to the visual art-forms, a formal distinction. They speak in terms of attributes such as: *mimetic,* imitative, realistic naturalistic styles, manners, forms and works; as opposed to *abstract*, informal, conceptual, constructive, analytic styles, manners, forms and works. This formal distinction is aproblematically employed to qualify the difference obtaining between classical or traditional and modern art and, futhermore, in order to define the boundaries of modern art. I would rather suggest that all art-forms and art-works, of all times, are essentially *abstract*, if they are art at all. Because art is not *reality:* it is neither a thing or object, nor a complex of things or objects.[8] Art is a celebration and interpretation of reality in totality, the world. The artness of art-works resides in the realm of *appearance*: *between* the real and the ideal, between the physical and the spiritual, between the facts and the intentions, between the given data and the imaginative projects.[9] To say that art is appearance[10] means to say that art is a *system of signs*.

5.ii Art-works are signs. The widest definition of a sign is: something that stands for something else. But, insofar as all things are signs, as semiotic would suggest, the specificity of those signs which we call art-works must be established and clarified. It would be confusing, if nothing else, to entertain the gratuitous thought that natural beings, artefacts, useful tools, mathematical and conventional symbols, letters of the alphabets and colours on the palette, the silence of my piano and the whisper of the wind, Picasso's *Guernica* and Schönberg's *A survivor from Warsaw,* and all art-works, are all signs in the same way. It would appear that art-works, unlike all other signs, are never exhausted by their vicarious role of signifying *something else*. They do not stand for something else. In other words, they are self-sufficient and self-justifying signs; organic and absolute signs.[11] They are, consequently, never exhausted in their energy and power to signify many things. They are *polysemic:* always open to new and further interpretations. Beauty includes the mentioned and specific properties of the art-works as signs that finally point to themselves.

6. If the beautiful artefact is a linguistic-semantic event, even a rudimentary analysis of the chain and process of communication, of the links of the chain and of the dialectical moments of the process, could prove to be fruitful and inspiring. We have the source of artistic communication: *the artist.* The artist is such insofar as he is human *in act:* insofar as he is sense-perceiving, thinking, loving. In his making according to art the artist effects operations which are synthetic and eminently expressive of the anthropological constitution as such. The artist operates, forms, according to what he is and in force of what he is.

7. The artist chooses *means and materials* with a view to the achievement of a teleological fulfilment of the materials and of himself; not only of himself as individual, but of himself as situated in a dialogical, linguistic, communicative chain and context. The artist teleologically fulfils *(finalises)* himself as a communicative and dialogical individual, that is: as a spiritual individual. Man the artist produces himself in producing signs. The means and materials are *the from which,*[12] the active-passive disposition. They are potential to the realisation of an idea which has been specifically, characteristically, constructively and ideally foreseen. The materials have, in themselves, a seminal manner of unfolding, of disposing themselves to the future possibilities of transformation and order-giving. The materials have in themselves a disposition which determines them and which determines the outcome of their possible transformations, the process of these transformations and the agent operating in this process. Clearly, the mentioned disposition and manner of unfolding cannot be ignored and neglected, even though it can itself be transformed, metamorphosed, even veiled, hidden and *inverted.*[13] The nature of the materials as *the from which* and *potential to* disposed in such or such manner, illumines the principle according to which the organic is the teleological, self-finalised; and conversely, that the teleo-

logical self-finalised is the organic. Only an adequate understanding of finality and teleology can ground an adequate understanding of reality.

8. The *significant content*, the signified, is the idea. The idea is the manifestation of reality, or thing, as reality really is; as reality is in truth. The idea is here understood also as the knowledge, even intuitive and pre-reflective knowledge, of the manifestation of the thing or reality as the reality of the thing truly is. The idea is, furthermore, the forming form: the principle *according to which,* in its widest sense.

8.i There are different sorts of ideas. There are what we should call *great* ideas: clear, comprehensive, synthetic visions of the world; profound and deep conceptions which sustain, permeate and constitute the edifice of a historical epoch, a culture and a civilisation. There are, on the other hand, what we may call *small* ideas or, after Plato, *idols(eidola).* The great ideas represent the universal destinies of mankind. When crystallised or sedimented in a particular *situation* [14] and when embodied in a characteristic event, great ideas produce great masterpieces: the mind, man's self-consciousness at each particular time, in its body. The great ideas are epochal ideas. They are as rare as the great epochs, cultures and civilisations. They nourish, nonetheless, the generation of the great masterpieces, the beautiful art-works, the most significant and the most characteristic of the many aspects of reality.

8.ii The great ideas are syntheses of the epochal *presuppositions,* of the prejudices and of the pre-knowledge which, again, constitute every conception of reality and of the world. Great ideas contain in themselves, as in a seed, all the aspects of man's self-consciousness and of man's consciousness of the world, of his world, in each particular epoch. They are necessary, inevitable, constitutive and dynamic. They represent and are the proper, adequate object of philosophy conceived as the science of the history of thought, of man's thought, of man situated in time. (Think of great ideas such as: the Greek idea of being and of the *cosmos*; the Medieval idea of reality as God's creation; the Renaissance idea of man's centrality, as *microcosm*, in the universe; the idea, prevailing in modern times, of the subjectively grounded certitude, and of the self-producing, self-determining self-consciousness; the idea, in the technological world, of reality as a universal and supreme result of *machination).*

8.iii The *small* ideas are echoes and reflexes of the great ideas. They are obscured by and encrusted with particularities, opinions, individual passions, psychological and emotional dispositions; in other words, with characters which obstruct the conscious grasping of the world and of the epochal forces which sustain and govern every manifestation of life at any given time in history. The small ideas live, parasitically, off the strength and in the shadow of the epochal ideas. They have the same epochal foundation, but lack the evocative, interpretative strength and universality which characterise the great ideas. The small ideas are ephemeral and do not stand the test of time and the judgement of tradition. They do not speak to us with the same force and evidence of the great ideas.

9. The *form*. We may even call it the signifier or the formed form. It is the exterior vestment and the soul's movement outward. It is the idea's process of self-expression in visible, sensible manifestations. The form is the order of means and materials. While the form lets the idea appear, it also embodies it. The adequate form is the technically *correct* form which fully corresponds to the particular idea, to its historical position in the entire tradition of ideas and of techniques, to the materials-means and to the stage of their historical development. The formed form is the adequate order of its adequate complexity.[15]

10. But if, as it happens so frequently nowadays, the receiver *does not understand,* if he/she is left disoriented and insecure when faced with an art-work, how could one then argue any more in favour of the semiological, significant and communicative nature of art and of art-works? Furthermore, the total or quasi-total state of confusion in which the criteria of taste and evaluation oscillate and are afloat seems to denounce precisely the loss of any possible, universally satisfactory criterion of aesthetic judgement. It seems clear that, in similar circumstances, the subjectivistic recourse to the so-called principle *de gustibus non est disputandum,* one should not and cannot argue on matters of taste, does not lead anywhere! To the contrary, the same recourse to the mentioned so-called principle stands already as a clear indication of a crisis of judgement, no less than of the bankruptcy situation, the insolvent conditions in which art floats. Rather than barricading oneself behind the gratuitous psychologistic position, one would find it much more useful and

much more fruitful to *abandon oneself* to the logic of the *thing* in question, and to examine the art-object through the analysis of its linguistic or semiotic elements. In other words, and in the context of this schema, one should try to reconstruct the process here suggested, from the number 6 to 9; perhaps more fruitfully from point 9. The signifier, the formed-form and the communicative process in its totality need to be de-coded and interpreted with a view to the illumination of the ideal meaning, of the significant signified, of the form and of the means and materials.

The understanding of an art-work is a matter of language. And every language must be known before it can be understood and before it may become expressive of the more subtle poetical, emotional and conceptual shades of meaning. As for *taste*, there is only one thing one could sensibly do with it: to *educate it* ![16]

11. The taste needs to be educated: not only the *external* taste attentive to the physical aspects of the art-works, not only the physical sensibility which finally digests, absorbs and retains material aspects of the art-work. One needs also, and foremost, to educate the taste of and for the organic and spiritual life of the beautiful artefact. This is the teleological taste, capable of grasping the development of the artistic idea in its technical and structural details of configuration.

11.i Practically one should question the epochal presuppositions and the context of the artefact. One should, in other words, situate the art-work in the spiritual context of its time. First and foremost, one should question the concept of truth that govern each particular work. Every art-work, we said earlier, just as every *world* presupposes a particular conception of truth, that is: a particular conception of reality. One should then search for the idea

11.ii by means of the recognition, at least provisional, intuitive, not yet justified nor reflected upon, of the formally significant event;

11.iii by means of the reconstruction of the order-giving and informing process which aims at *ad-equating* the means and the materials to the formal goals. Such a reconstruction or re-creation should finally reveal how successfully the process of ordination and information of means and materials is really adequate to the formal expression of a great idea.

Aristotle's Poetics and Aesthetics

All art deals with bringing something into existence.

Aesthetics, as the discipline which investigates, with the tools and methods of reflective thinking, the nature and the meaning of what we call *art*, in all its aspects, is a *modern* invention. It is a discipline which, as a systematic endeavour, could have only been born within the horizon of subjective thinking, finally grown to maturity in Hegel's philosophy. Indeed, as Hegel puts it in his *Vorlesungen über die Aesthetik:*

> Even the work of art, in which the mind objectifies itself, belongs to the realm of conceptual thought. By considering it scientifically, the mind is only fulfilling the demands of its innermost nature. In fact, (...), the mind is properly and adequately satisfied only when it has penetrated with its thought all the products of its own activity.1

Although the thematisation of aesthetics as an autonomous discipline is of recent origin, we find the foundation of the Western philosophy of art, aesthetics and indeed of Western philosophy *tout court,* in Greek thought. I will suggest that Aristotle's doctrine, in particular, provides us with some deeply incisive, insightful and fundamental categories, and a model which constitutes, to my mind, the condition of possibility for a definition of *art,* of the *work of art* and even of the *aesthetic experience.* Furthermore, despite Aristotle's ontological *Weltanschauung, prejudice* and presuppositions, his meditations on art, rare and unsystematic as they are, can help us to bridge the difference between classic, ontological, traditional and pre-Cartesian thinking, on the one hand, and the subjective, man-centred, modern and contemporary thought, on the other hand.

I would initially hope to disprove the statement by one of the greatest contemporary historians of aesthetics, namely W. Tatarkiewicz, who expressed, in a rather disconcerting manner, the following opinion: "The antique concept of art was clear and well defined, but it no longer corresponds to present day requirements. It is a historical relic".2

22

It is by now well known that the concept or idea of art has been, perhaps more so than any other philosophical concept or idea, subjected to a virtually unending variety of treatments and has constituted one of the most controversial themes of philosophical discussion. That discussion, as we know it, gained enormous momentum in the Nineteenth century, thanks to the impact determined by German Idealism. The discussion has further gained exuberant and indeed excessive proportions in our century, stimulated and challenged as it is by newly opened horizons of creative and *poetic* possibilities in the practice of the arts. Even in more recent years, we witness the abundance of attempts at re-awakening and re-formulating the centuries-old question: What is art? That question appears, to most, to be intractable and resilient to the methods of philosophy considered as clear and distinct thinking.

How could one provide an answer to such a question, capable of encompassing, containing and accounting for the diversity of the subject-matter, i.e. art? And we should note that the polysemic denotation of the word *art* unfolds itself both synchronically and diachronically. *Art* means all art-forms, all works of art, styles, artists, receivers, etc., at any one given point in time, on the one hand, and it also means all the different periods, epochs, cultures, with their artistic experiences and with their philosophical doctrines that interpreted those experiences, thus telling us what was meant by *art*.

The problem of the philosophical definition of art implies at least two, mostly forgotten and overshadowed, deeper questions, namely: What is *philosophy?*, and: what is a *definition?* Because, finally, any conception of art just as any *experience* of art, both in its making and in its reception, presuppose a conception of truth.[3] I shall not explicitly deal with either of the mentioned deeper questions in this context, nor indeed shall I deal directly or thematically with the problem of the definition, that is of the adequate and all-inclusive definition of art.

It seems to me that all those who argue against the possibility of defining art, do so, finally, on two accounts. Firstly because of the historical dimension of art and the polysemy of this word which is doubtless applied to a virtually innumerable variety of human experiences and the virtually countless facets of each one of these prismatic experiences. The second account is the one never quite settled and never brought to balance, namely the account of the nature of philosophy in general, its adequacy to deal with art, the general problem of hermeneutical interpretation as a way of explaining the relationship obtaining between philosophy, art and other spiritual experiences historically sedimented.

With reference to the historicity of art and the problem of its definition, I believe it was Friedrich Nietzsche who argued, in one of his not all too rare moments of critical disposition towards Idealism, that no definition of art could be given; for no definition could be given of anything the very essence of which is constituted by historicity. I confess that I fail to understand what precisely Nietzsche meant by *definition*. He had no liking for definitions, anyway!

It seems quite clear to me that, by and large, traditional considerations and reflections on art inherited the Platonic and Neo-Platonic assumption according to which art is the realm of participated beauty, where beauty itself is considered as a metaphysically transcendent and hypostatically divine paradigm. That tradition reached its maturity, even though translated into terms of subjectivity, in Hegel's philosophy, whose aesthetics is articulated as the science of man-made beauty, and further survived in all the projects on aesthetics that define themselves as philosophy of beauty. On the other hand, we have witnessed, particularly in this century, the emergence of what could be called a reborn form of nominalism. Frustrated by the difficulties of defining, once and for all, in a logically, clinically, and linguistically justifiable manner the concept of beauty and the concept of art, the mentioned nominalistic and conventionalist trend would argue that *L'arte è tutto ciò che gli uomini chiamano arte*.[4] This approach is particularly favoured by sympathisers of analytic philosophy, and is partially grounded on Wittgenstein's a-historical conception and analyses of language. According to this view, beauty could not be adequately defined nor logically explained; it could only be privately employed as a connotational word, in particular circumstances. It would follow, from this position, that a definition of aesthetics as *the science of the beautiful* is finally nonsensical. Even more, it is no definition at all. By the same token, any definition, or attempt at a definition, of art, which were to employ the word *beauty* as a part of the definition, would equally be nonsensical, *qua* definition, and finally, again, left to the whim of the private, subjectivistic, unwarranted and circumstantial interpretations.

But let us now return to Aristotle and his conception of art. I will limit myself to suggest an interpretation of some few relevant texts by the philosopher concerning *techne* and *poiesis*. We are, of course, aware of the fact that these words had for the Greeks, and for Aristotle, a wide meaning or extension. They meant all arts and crafts. However, and particularly so in Aristotle, we can read the more specific meaning of the word as denoting the activity of the artist. (It must be noted that in Plato's *Republic* we already find the distinction between the crafts-man or *demiourgos,* and the artist/imitator-of-imitations, or *technites.*)

> All art deals with bringing something into existence; and to pursue an art means to study how to bring into existence a thing which may either exist or not, and the efficient cause of which lies in the maker and not in the thing made; for art does not deal with things that come to existence of necessity or according to nature, since these have their *arche (principle)* in themselves.5

This statement grants us an initial insight into Aristotle's way of approaching the question of art. Aristotle is concerned with the activity and the process that constitute and bring to light the object *artefact.* "Aesthetic investigation may be centred either in the concept of beauty or the concept of art. While Plato gave priority to the concept of beauty", Aristotle, according to Zeller, "at the beginning of his *Poetics* has put aside the concept of beauty and launched upon the study of art".6

The mentioned Aristotelian passage defines art as a mode of extrinsic production. Insofar as produced from without, the work of art possesses and manifests less of being. It is not self-constitutive, it does not immanently abide by itself and does not come to the light of presence in force of an immanent interaction of all its causes. In other words, it lacks the substantial perfection of *physis* (nature) i.e. of the self-unfolding process from itself to itself; and it lacks the perfection, immanent and divine of *praxis* both ethical and epistemic. It would seem, therefore, that, if we viewed the question of the nature of the work of art in the light of Aristotle's general schema of the categorical constitution of the universe, the *ousia* (substance), so to speak, of the artefact cannot be found in itself, immanently, but must be looked for in the *hyle* or the disposition of the materials from which the work is made, and in the *eidos* in man's soul, which produces the transformation of the natural material into the cultural, informed product. The work of art would then be a quasi-*ousia* (a quasi-substance). But this is only part of the whole story, and indeed an episode worth developing and clarifying.

Although other than *physis,* although other than immanent and substantial processes, *techne/poiesis* proceeds, like nature, towards an appointed goal. Indeed art imitates nature.7 Art produces from without, by proceeding in a fashion analogous of the *doing,* the immanent self-unfolding of *physis* . It strives to become, as it were, an organic and immanent process or activity. Art could then be called a quasi-*energeia.* It is a mimetic *energeia* (active autonomous substance). The theme of *mimesis* is, however, much more complex and indeed much more rich of suggestions, and I shall return to it in chapter five. I understand that, when Aristotle insists on *mimesis* as the determining element of artistic activity, he does so with a view to grounding the autonomous and quasi-substantial character of the work of art. Of course, every art/craft proceeds, like *physis, mimesising* nature, towards a goal, just as *physis* itself does.

Techne/poiesis, in other words, can produce useful artefacts. It would then aim at, foreground and intentionalise the function of the useful artefact. Even in this *techne/poiesis mimesises* nature. But only insofar as it proceeds towards a goal, and a *functional goal,* according to a certain order of formation, information and activation of means and materials.

Even in this, of course, both art and craft *mimesise praxis,* but only insofar as they follow the direction of an organic and spiritual process that begins in man's soul.[8] Art then would *mimesise* in view of and in function of the artefact *qua* useful. *Mimesis,* in other words, would only be itself in function of the product. It would be the means to the realisation of its appointed functional purpose. In the more specific sense, however, *poiesis,* as discussed in the context of the *Poetics* and of the *Rhetoric, mimesises* in the sense that, instead of aiming at a functional goal, first and foremost it aims at exhibiting characters and features that foreground the very form of the artefact: its order, its symmetry, its beauty, its uselessness, its being-as-*physis* and *praxis,* its being-as immanent energy and a substantial *entelecheia.*

If this is so, *mimesis* has to be understood as itself the very goal and aim of the poetic or artistic making; and the product of art should be understood as made first and foremost as *mimesis* of the *energetic* and *substantial* order of being: that is total, measured, ordered, proportioned, and *teleion (finalised).* And this is what we call *artistic form* and *beauty.*

Apart from being self-sufficient or, better, quasi-self-sufficient, i.e. while being a goal in itself and beyond the constrictions of utility and functionality,[9] the beautiful artefact is constituted as an *analogical syn-*

thesis of many perfections. In this respect, the artefact is better and greater than real objects. As Aristotle puts it:

> the superiority of handsome men, so it is said, over plain men and the works of the painter's art over the real objects, really consists in this, that a number of scattered good points have been collected together into one example...10

This suggestion points to what in contemporary aesthetics is called the *polysemy*, the *open-ness*, the inexhaustibility, finally the *ambiguity* of the work of art, and the virtually infinite possibility of its interpretations or fruitions.

Furthermore, insofar as poetry mimesises "what may happen, what is possible according to the law of probability and necessity",[11] we can understand that art either mimesises nature or perfects it by reaching goals that *physis* could never realise.[12] The work of art, therefore, is constituted as the *sign* of the real, of the ideal, of the possible, of the utopic image of a more perfect spiritual world. Thus, reading Aristotle, I can understand in a deeper manner the contemporary claims and suggestions that the work of art is an event of *co-reality(Mit-realität)*, as M. Bense and other phenomenologists (not forgetting J.P. Sartre) would put it; that it is an occurrence of the *immanence de valeur* and of the *plénitude d'être*, of which M. Dufrenne eloquently and elegantly writes. It is the *pure presence*, an incident of *pure visibility*, the triumphant, undisturbed luminosity of the *form*; it is finally what, with C. Brandi, we could call an instance of the *astanza*, another word to suggest the idea of self-revealing, autonomous, stable presence.

In concluding this chapter, I want to make some final remarks that may suggest some final analogical motifs to be found both in Aristotle's works and in a particular trend of contemporary aesthetics, namely the semiological investigations of the formalist school.[13] I return, here, to some central ideas already outlined in the previous chapter, that will be reiterated throughout this text.

We have become increasingly aware of what Prof. Lohmann has pregnantly called the *linguistic constitution of the world*. The mind, with its ability to inform and transform nature, was born when a first humanoid *saw something as something else:* the stone on a beach as the flint; the branch as a weapon; the fur as clothing; the word as the concept...This, as I understand it, is *mimesis*.

As we have already seen in the introductory chapter, in the splendid Homeric Hymn to the God, Hermes, when still a child, walked out of the cave and met the tortoise. At its sight "he gained endless delight", he laughed, for he had seen the humble creature as something else: the musical instrument, the lyre. Hermes embodies the experience of language, of sign-processes, of *techne,* of artistic invention and creation. *He saw nature as culture.* He transformed the tortoise into music. Later in the poem he is referred to as the *inventor of the art of making fire* . And later in time, through the centuries, he became the god of articulate speech and the god of interpretation. The making of signs is already the act of creative hermeneutics.

If works of art are *signs,* they are nonetheless distinguishable from all other signs in the universal economy of language, because of some precise characters that semiology likes to call: *self-reference* and *polysemic ambiguity.* To my mind, both determinations are already implicit in Aristotle's thoughtful meditations. As self-referential, the sign that is the work of art points to itself, is viewed and contemplated for its own sake; it is beautiful, in the wide sense of the word, i.e. as attracting to its very presence, immanently and totally. The self-reference however is triggered, warranted and sustained by the unfamiliar, gratuitous, ambiguous and polysemic structure of the sign that is the work of art. But although this somehow explains or elucidates the nature of the aesthetic experience and the aesthetic properties of a given sign, more is needed so that the aesthetic object may be called a *work of art* in the more rigorous and more demanding meaning of the word. The self-referential and ambiguous message is properly and fully a work of art when it compels me to read in it and through it, indeed with it, an image of the world, a cultural content, a spiritual experience, an ideal value. Whether real or possible, probable or ideal, that image cannot avoid being the project of a future order of the world to be brought to light and to be realised.

Aristotle on Diction and Tragedy

Language serves a man not only to express something but also to express himself

This chapter intends to comment on a central concept in Aristotle's *Poetics* and show the importance of an adequate understanding of *lexis*, also with reference to contemporary literary theories, in order to grasp fully the essence of tragedy, in particular, and of literary diction, in general.

Lexis has been treated considerably by Aristotle in two of his works: the *Art of Rhetoric* and the *Poetics* where its first mention occurs at the beginning of chapter 6 in the very definition of tragedy, and as one of the six constitutive ingredients of tragedy itself. Interestingly, though confusing and uncomfortable for any attempt at chronological order, the two works refer to each other on numerous occasions. Furthermore, the treatment of the general theory of *lexis* consistently and extensively overlaps in the two mentioned works.

The scholarly treatment of *lexis,* within the context of the *Poetics,* has been neglected and not sufficiently understood, especially in the late Eighteenth and Nineteenth centuries. I would venture to suggest that this neglect can be interpreted as a corollary phenomenon, in the wake of the disrepute into which rhetoric, understood and practised as a thesaurus of figures of speech and a handbook of readymade formulae, had fallen. Partly responsible for the reduction of the science of rhetoric to the state of an oratorial recipe book, were the Italian Renaissance commentators of Aristotle, exposed as they were to the fusion of Aristotelian and Roman (especially Horatian) rhetorical practices, while at once stressing the importance and foregrounding the function of *elocutio, ornatus, decorum, convenientia,* in other words: the elegance of diction *avant tout.*[1] We could also suggest that the aesthetic sensibility of post-Romanticism in the last century, favouring the conception of art as free expression of the creative subjectivity of the genius, could not but fail to pay adequate attention to technical aspects of diction and its contrived labours.

In chapter 6 of his *Poetics,* Aristotle provides us with a definition of tragedy:

> Tragedy is, then, a representation of an action that is heroic and complete and of a certain magnitude, by means of language enriched with all kinds of ornament, each used separately in the different parts of the play: it represents men in action and does not use narrative, and through pity and fear it effects relief of these and similar emotions.2

Although the word *lexis* does not appear in this passage, we are given a first indication of its role and function when we read: "by means of language enriched with all kinds of ornament". Interestingly, in this otherwise very compressed passage the reference to enriched language is promptly elaborated by a relatively generous qualification:

> By "language enriched" I mean that which has rhythm and tune, i.e. song, and by "the kinds separately" I mean that some effects are produced by verse alone and some again by song.3

It may seem strange perhaps that of all the elements in his definition of tragedy, *pleasing language* is the only one to which Aristotle pays immediate attention. We detect a sense of urgency in Aristotle's hastened qualification. And, indeed, what follows shortly after the definition, highlights this point. Here we find the first explicit mention of *lexis:*

> Since the representation is performed by living persons, it follows at once that one essential part of tragedy is the spectacular effect and, besides that, song-making and diction. For these are the means of representation. By diction(*lexis)* I mean the metrical arrangement of words.4

This definition of *lexis,* too particular and too specialised, will be further qualified and illustrated in other passages which I shall examine later. My first concern is to establish the unquestionable importance and value attributed by Aristotle to *diction.* Shortly after the quoted text, the philosopher mentions the six parts that constitute and make up a tragedy:

> Necessarily, then, every tragedy has six constitutive parts, and on these its quality depends. They are plot, character, diction, thought, spectacle, and song. Two of these are the means of representation: one is the manner: three are the objects represented. This list is exhaustive, and practically all poets employ these elements, for every drama includes alike spectacle and character and plot and diction and song and thought.5

Each of these elements or parts, as it is well known, is treated with considerably different degrees of attention by Aristotle. Thought, spectacle and song are only minimally explained. To *action*, which is the soul of the plot, just as plot is the principle and soul of tragedy, Aristotle devotes only minimal explanatory comments in the *Poetics*, thus provoking considerable confusion in the mind of those commentators who fail to make reference to Aristotle's ethical writings where *praxis* is adequately analysed and clarified.[6] Plot and its correlative element, character, are referred to more frequently. Diction is, by far, the element most amply and more extensively dealt with.

Philologists and commentators of the *Poetics* have not failed to notice the disproportionate and (according to some) even excessive and unjustifiable attention paid by Aristotle to *lexis,* especially in chapters 19-22.[7] Despairing to provide, within the limits of this chapter, an adequate account of the state of philological research on the problem of *lexis,* I will limit myself to presenting a selected number of random examples that may illustrate the prejudices, the misapprehension and perhaps confusion suffered by some commentators. During the last century Ritter questioned, doubted and contested the authenticity of chapter 20 of the *Poetics,* while Steinthal doubted the authenticity of the three chapters, 20-22, dealing with *lexis.* In this century, Solmsen suspect, in a less extreme fashion, that these chapters might be, if authentic, later interpolations.[8] In his otherwise significant study, Bignami has nothing to say about *lexis,* seized as he is by Romantic and Idealistic enthusiasm and preoccupied with establishing the ideal cosmic nature of art.[9] Valgimigli, who has produced one of the most scholarly and attractive commentaries on the *Poetics,* well complemented by an enlightening introduction, in a shortened edition of his work decided to *suppress* chapters 20-22.[10]

If unwarranted and inexcusable is Valgimigli's decision to omit and leave aside the mentioned chapters on *lexis,* I find it singularly gratuitous that G. Else, in his extensive, detailed and scrupulous commentary, should have repeated Valgimigli's mistake.[11] Else, to begin, had no reason to be concerned with lack of space as in a small edition. In fact, having treated with abundance of commentary every concept and every argument in the *Poetics,* at page 567, confronted with the chapters on *lexis,* Else seems to lose heart:

> The three and one-half chapters(including the second half of chapter 19) which deal with *lexis* are omitted from this study for three reasons: 1) they are technical to a very high degree (especially chapters 20 and 21) and bristle with special problems, so that any cogent discussion of them would have to be inordinately long and complex; 2) to a degree unequalled by any other part of the work they have to be considered (again chapters 20 and 21 particularly) in a special context, that of the development of *grammatical* study in Greece; and (3) they have very little, astonishingly little, connection with any other part of Aristotle's poetry.[12]

I confess my dissatisfaction especially with the third reason: that the chapters in question "have very little, astonishingly little, connection with any other part of Aristotle's theory of poetry". I disagree with Else and rather ask: is not *lexis* understood to be one of the six constitutive parts of tragedy? More basically, could a tragedy, or any other literary genre, come to be and persist in being without its diction and linguistic articulation?

Lexis has been variously translated as: *sprachliche Ausdruch, Rede, elocution, language, style, diction, verbal structure,* and otherwise. Not all equally adequate and clear translations, some are clearly confusing. V.Goldschmidt has noted the difficulty in translation:

> The difficulty of translation that the word lexis presents, comes from the fact that it denotes, at once, verbal expression in general (as in ch. 25), everyday speech (1459 a 12), finally and specifically style (R., III, 1, 1404 a 26, 28-29).[13]

To avoid the probable restriction of meaning which modern vocabulary may impose upon *lexis,* I shall quote the second definition given by Aristotle:

> The fourth of the literary elements is *lexis.* By this I mean, as we said above, the expression of meaning in words (and this is essentially the same in verse and prose).[14]

In the fifth chapter (*La Diction*) of *L'esthétique d'Aristote*[15] Svoboda notes the neglect suffered by Aristotle's aesthetics of language:

> And in the *Poetics* (chs. 19-22) and in the *Rhetoric* (III, 1, 1404 a 5-19), there are some, often neglected, detailed and interesting considerations concerning the aesthetics of language. (...) As regards poetry, Aristotle attributes great importance to the diction; it is considered one of the six elements of tragedy.[16]

V. Goldschmidt, in his compressed treatment of lexis, is equally convinced of the decisive function fulfilled by *lexis* in the poetics:

> One sees then that the stylistic work contributes in a decisive manner to the understanding of the tragic poem: the style manifests concretely the essence of tragedy and contributes, for to use the Hegelian expression, "the sensible manifestation of the idea.17

Encouraged by the work of the fore-mentioned authors, I shall submit a seminal and brief analysis of *lexis,* in the form of a reading of chs. 19-22 of the *Poetics,* in particular, with some unavoidable references to the *Rhetoric.* I shall leave aside ch. 19 (1456 b 8ff.) where *lexis,* as vehicle of *dianoia (thought),* denotes in a selective manner *hypokritike* or elocution, the art of delivery. This denotation is strongly redolent of conventional oratorial preoccupations and, with reference to tragedy, points to the art of delivery that belongs to good actors, the skill of movingly convincing recitation. I shall also leave aside ch. 20 where Aristotle gives a compressed compendium of grammatical aspects and functions of words. The passage relevant to our inquiry into the essence of *lexis* occurs in ch. 21 (1447 b 3-4):

> Every noun is either ordinary or rare or metaphorical or ornamental or invented or lengthened or curtailed or altered.

This list of types of nouns, elements and basic ingredients of *lexis,* that seem to aspire to completeness, is further qualified by a distinction that divides all nouns into two classes. In Aristotle's words:

> An ordinary word is one used by everybody, a rare word one used by some.

The arguments that follow focus on a particular rare use of words, namely metaphor. Though well known, the definition of metaphor is worthy of recollection:

> Mctaphor is the application of a strange(different) term either transferred from the genus to the species or from the species and applied to the genus, or from one species to another or else by analogy. (1457 b 6).

Metaphor, therefore, consists in *epiphora:* transposing onto a thing a name that denotes something else. Its logical and metaphysical substratum is identifiable with analogy. Sign of a natural gift, *the greatest power by far* (1459 a 7; 1455 a 33), the ability to invent metaphors is also the mark of a philosophical disposition:

> As we have said before, metaphors should be drawn from objects that are
> somewhat related, but not obviously related; just as, for instance, in philosophy
> it needs sagacity to grasp similarity in things that are apart. (1412 a 11 & 13).

At the beginning of the eleventh chapter of the *Rhetoric,* we read that
the characteristic power of metaphor consists in *setting things before the
eyes.* Metaphors reveal to us more of reality and, indeed, in a quite
novel fashion, they expand our knowledge of the world. They make
things come to a new life. They foreground reality.

I shall return to this point, by linking it to the experience of *wonder*,
and to some salient features of tragedy. But I must first pay attention to
another passage, in the *Poetics,* which is particularly worthy of notice
for in it a connection can be established between the function of
metaphors and other types of *strange* and unfamiliar diction. In this passage, Aristotle's insight into the nature of poetic language and of literary diction proves once again its unerring wisdom. The lengthy passage
that follows, in its extraordinary originality, shows Aristotle's superi-
ority over his predecessors and sounds as a statement of cogent actuality:

> The merit of diction is to be clear and not to be commonplace. The clearest dic-
> tion is that made up of ordinary words, but it is commonplace. (...) That which
> employs unfamiliar words is dignified and outside the common usage. By
> *unfamiliar* I mean a rare word, a metaphor, a lengthening and anything beyond
> the ordinary use. But if a poet writes entirely in such words, the result will be
> either a riddle or jargon; if made up of metaphors, a riddle and if of rare words,
> jargon. The essence of a riddle consists in describing a fact by an impossible
> combination of words. (...) A medley of rare words is jargon. We need, then, a
> mixture of the two. For the one kind will save the diction from being prosaic
> and commonplace: the rare word, for example, and the metaphor and the
> *ornament:* whereas the ordinary words give clarity. (...) Now, to make an
> obtrusive use of this licence is ridiculous: but moderation is a requisite common
> to all kinds of writing.18

Diction must be clear, familiar, recognisable, hence readily decodable,
on the one hand. However, a diction qualified solely by these attributes
would be commonplace and prosaic. We would have clarity of communication but an uninteresting lack of information. On the other hand,
diction could be articulated as a structure of rare, strange and unpre-
dictable orders. In this case we would have what Aristotle calls *barbarism,* jargon: a private dialect bordering on obscure, cryptic, meaningless noise. If the extreme strangeness were sustained by a relentless
use of metaphorical devices, we would have *enigmas,* riddles and unde-
codable puzzles. The poetically effective diction cannot be prosaic lan-

guage, nor can it be a private, incommunicable dialect or jargon. The clarity of ordinary diction, sustained by familiarity and community of code or convention, can avoid the commonplace and, hence, produce poetic utterances only when adequately mixed or combined with rare, unfamiliar, unexpected, metaphorical ingredients. Centuries before the findings of structuralism, linguistics, formalism, semiotics, Aristotle has clearly suggested that the work of art, the aesthetic message, the pleasure of reading, the delight of discovery or *having things set before our eyes*, the epistemic value of artistic messages, are the result of highly informative (because ambiguous) *wonderful* (1460 a 11ff.), surprising, estranging diction, within a context of recognisable ingredients. The effective poetic diction is structured as symbiotic interaction of familiarity and unfamiliarity, of estrangement, violation, deviation and the obvious, the rule, the norm:

> For instance, Aeschylos and Euripides wrote the same iambic line with the change of one word only, a rare word instead of one made ordinary by custom, yet the one line seems beautiful and the other trivial. "The ulcer eats the flesh of this my foot", and Euripides instead of "eats" put "feasts upon". (1448 b 19).

All the essential elements of effective diction: clarity and rarity, familiarity and violation or deviation, satisfied and surprised expectation, wonder and the pleasure of learning, are perfectly contained in a sublime passage of the *Rhetoric:*

> Most smart sayings are derived from metaphor, and also from misleading the hearer beforehand. For it becomes more evident to him that he has learnt something, when the conclusion turns out contrary to his expectation, and the mind seems to say: "How true it is! but I missed it." And smart apophthegms arise from not meaning what one says as in the apophthegm of Stesicorous, that "the grasshoppers will sing to themselves from the ground".
> And clever riddles are agreeable for the same reason: for something is learnt, and the expression is also metaphorical. And what Theodorus calls "novel expressions" arise when what follows is paradoxical and, as he puts it, not in accordance with our previous expectation; just as humorists make use of slight changes in words. The same effect is produced by jokes that turn on a change of letters, for they are deceptive. These novelties occur in poetry as well as in prose. For instance, the following verse does not finish as the hearer expects: "and he strode on under his feet / chilblains", whereas the hearer thought he was going to say "sandals". (1422 a 12 ff).

Thanks to Russian Formalism and the Prague school, not to mention semiotics, it is universally accepted that a message assumes a poetic function or, more precisely, an *aesthetic* function when ambiguous and self-focused. As the quoted passage eloquently suggests, Aristotle had already reached the same conclusion, thus proving extraordinary insight into the nature of *lexis* and the manifold virtualities of language.

Aristotle's text could be clarified by adopting the language of semiotics. A characteristic of the aesthetic texts singled out by the Russian formalists is the so-called *device of making it strange:* in order to describe something which the addressee may have seen and recognised many times, the author unexpectedly uses words in a different way. One's first reaction is a sense of bewilderment, of being almost unable to recognise the object. Somehow the change in expressive device also changes the content. Thus art increases difficulty and the duration of perception and describes the object as if one were seeing it for the first time so that the aim of the image is not to bring closer to our understanding the meaning it conveys, but to create a particular perception of the object. This explains the poetic use of archaisms, the difficulty and obscurity of artistic creations when presented for the first time to an audience as yet unprepared for them, or those violations which art brings into play at the very moment when one expects obedience to the customary golden rules:

> In art there is order and yet there is not a single column of a Greek temple that follows this order exactly, and aesthetic rhythm consists of a prosaic rhythm that has been violated (...). It is a question not of a complex rhythm, but a violation of that rhythm and such that it cannot be predicted. If violation becomes the rule, it loses the force that it had as an operational obstacle.[19]

In tragedy, the estranged diction, the enigmatic *lexis* foregrounded against a background of familiar names, myths, experiences, laws and social conventions, is in function of the plot, the character, the action: themselves riddles and enigmas immersed in a fluid dialectics of ambiguities and conflicts.[20]

In one of his numerous gratifying pages of *La Struttura Assente,* Umberto Eco, draws an analogy between aesthetic message and tragic plot, allowing the full meaning and function of *lexis* to emerge. Having defined the message with aesthetic function as that which is structured in an ambiguous and unfamiliar, rare way with reference to that system of expectation that is the code, Eco comments:

> What happens to the aesthetic message is the same as what happens to tragic plot according to the precepts of Aristotelian poetics: the plot must make happen something that surprises us, something that goes beyond our expectations and therefore *para ten doxan* (contrary to common opinion). But to ensure that this event be accepted and that we may identify with it, it is necessary that, while

appearing incredible, it obeys, at once, some conditions of credibility; it must be endowed with a certain versimilitude. It is wondrous, strange and incredible that a son returns home after long years of war and wants to kill most savagely his mother, with the help and encouragement of his sister. (Confronted with a fact so contrary to any expectation, the spectator will grow tense, shocked by the ambiguous informational power of the extraordinary situation.). The event, however, must be credible and probable, lest it be rejected as pure madness: indeed, the son intends to kill his mother because she had induced her lover to kill her husband.21

In Aristotle's reflections on poetry and on tragedy, *lexis* focuses on, lets emerge and, more so, reconstitutes within itself, in its ambiguous familiarity, the riddles of human existence, the conflicts of Greek culture. It is through the power of *lexis* that we see, understand and re-enact the tragic action: stretched as it is between existence and destiny, ancient and new legality, myth and rationality, *physis* and *nomos,* nature and law, spontaneity and taboo. Through tragedy and its fundamentally ambiguous diction, we participate in the rediscovery of the origins of social life understood as linguistic experience. As spectators (or readers), caught between the forces and the characters in conflict, we, like the chorus, cannot choose or decide for one or the other. We cannot step back and remove ourselves from the conflict. In the end, because of the power of diction, we cease to be mere spectators. We enter another order of reality: the world of art. We are compelled to see that *many things are strange.*

Aristotle's Concept of Mimesis

L'arte e` una cosa mentale. (Art is a mental thing).

(Leonardo)

The artist must imitate that which is within the thing, that which is active through form and figure, and discourses to us - the Naturgeist or spirit of nature. (Coleridge)

Nature imitates art. (O. Wilde)

The very concept of *imitative*, *mimetic* and *realist* art has been exposed, in recent decades and in the light of contemporary artistic experiences, to serious criticism. In more general terms, we could even say that no other aesthetic concept is discussed as much as the concept of mimesis and imitation. The whole Western tradition has treasured and elaborated the meaning of this aesthetic category, and has recognised the central role played by it in the reflections on art by Plato and Aristotle.

All modern art, born as it is from the reaction against realist and representative art, and grounded upon a new conception of nature or reality, on the one hand, and of the artist's functions and operations, on the other hand, has exasperated its negative stance against imitation. Indeed, such a prejudicial and polemical position has forced the artist's subjectivity, all too often constrained by the paradox of *methodic solipsism*, to enormous abuses and to extremely one-sided statements. The concept of imitation and of realistic representation in art is furiously negated and passionately substituted by its extreme counter-concepts of abstractivism and of chemically pure formalism. Similar positions, in the sphere of artistic experiences as much as in the context of aesthetic discourse, are, to my mind, basically motivated, to begin, by the misunderstanding that traditional or classic art was in fact a *realist, representational* and *imitative* art.

The recent phenomenological theories[1] and the abundant semiotic studies[2] in particular seem, to date, to have sufficiently foregrounded and unequivocally clarified the mental, imaginary nature and the semiotic nature of art, hence its essential independence of reality conceived as *object, datum* and *res estensa*. Art, we could say, is considered to be an a-priori function of the human mind, and a culturally contrived expression of the same.

In general, even though in various degrees, Plato and Aristotle are commonly held responsible for the errors, the limitations and the inadequacy of mimetic realism in art. It must also be said that, despite the abundance of scholarly analyses aiming at clarifying the concept of *mimesis*, we are far from having fully accepted and unquestionably agreed upon the adequate understanding of the same concept as it occurs in Aristotle's works in particular.[3]

With reference to Plato, I can only briefly suggest that to say that the work of art imitates the copy of the idea: useful artefacts or natural beings, means also to say, at once, that the idea illumines, informs and comes to light in the mimetic work.[4] *Mimesis*, therefore, must be understood as the dialectical interaction between the copy and the model, the phenomenon and truth, the manifested and the manifesting *aletheia*. The work of art is a manifestation of ideal truth, no matter how weak. It belongs to the idea. Consequently, not even in Plato's doctrine can *mimesis* be totally and exclusively understood as the mere act of copying or the passive *holding the mirror up to nature*. Finally, the paradox must be recalled whereby the deceitful and lying mimetic arts must, for the ancient Greeks and particularly according to Plato, educate, which means to say that "the poet must bring to light the ideal dimension of what is beyond the given reality", to quote N. Hartmann.[5] Nonetheless, Plato's metaphysical conception of truth and reality as universal, transcendent and separate ideas, implies that *mimesis* signifies and articulates a rapport of dependence of nature and of useful artefacts upon the eternal ideas, and of artistic artefacts upon the former.[6]

According to Plato, *mimesis* relates the human arts to the prototypical archetype or idea. *Mimesis* is conceived as in function of the transcendent paradigm.[7]

In the analyses that follow, I suggest that Aristotle, in a quite original manner, conceived *mimesis*: 1. as an activity in itself and as a process,[8] 2. more precisely, especially in the context of his *Poetics*, as a specific determination of a particular type of *techne/poiesis*, namely the production of poets and artists in general,[9] 3. as in function of the objects it *imitates,* namely *physis* (nature) and *praxis* (action); where these "objects" are no longer understood, as according to Plato, to be transcendent and separate. By philological analysis and hermeneutic reconstruction of some of Aristotle's central arguments, I hope to clarify the philosopher's concept of *mimesis.*[10]

The discussion of our problem could aptly begin with the paraphrase of an expression particularly dear to our philosopher. Like being itself, like reality, also *mimesis is spoken and thought of in many ways.* Indeed the polysemy of the word reminds us of the difficulty of the problem at hand. in the *Poetica* (1460b 8) we read:

> The poet, being an imitator, like a painter or any other artist, must of necessity imitate one of three objects: things as they were or are, things as they are said or thought to be, or things as they ought to be.[11]

In the light of this text it would be quite difficult, if not even impossible, to deny that *mimesis* is also understood as imitation, copying and miming, in the very sense of actually representing, picturing and re-enacting a given state of affairs.[12] It would, however, be equally difficult if not even more difficult, to reduce the concept of *mimesis* to the mere notion of passive copy. Furthermore, the following analyses and interpretive remarks will suggest that the primary and essential meaning of *mimesis,* particularly in the context of the *Poetica*, is other and quite more significant than that of copy and imitation.

In his *Ethica Nicomachea* (EN, 1140a 1ff), the philosopher draws the essential distinction between *techne/poiesis* (making/producing) and *praxis* (action/doing):

> Making is different from doing (...) Nor is one of them a part of the other, for doing is not a form of making, nor making a form of doing.[13]

The difference is better qualified and explained in the following terms:

> All art deals with bringing something into existence; and to pursue an art means to study how to bring into existence a thing which may either exist or not, and the efficient cause *(arche)* of which lies in the maker and not in the thing made; for art does not deal with things that exist or come into existence of necessity, or according to nature *(physei)*, since these have their efficient cause in themselves.

I shall soon announce and discuss the theme of *physis* (nature). Let us, for the moment, pursue Aristotle's definition and qualification of *techne/poiesis* (art/craft/making) as they emerge from the opposition to the concept of *praxis* (action/doing). At *EN*, 1140b 1ff, Aristotle clarifies the nature of *phronesis* (prudence/practical judgement) which he clearly identifies with *praxis* and, at once, distinguishes from and opposes to both *techne* and *poiesis*.

> *Phronesis* is not the same as science. Nor can it be the same as art. It is not science, because matters of conduct admit of variation; and not art, because doing (*praxis*) and making (*poiesis*) are generically different, since making aims at an end distinct from the act of making, whereas in doing the end cannot be other than the act itself: doing well is itself the end.14

Making is therefore understood as a transient, transitive and extrinsic activity: its principle (*arche*) lies in the maker, it goal (*telos*) lies without the maker and his activity of making. In the case of action/doing (*praxis*) and of prudence/practical judgement (*phronesis*) on the contrary, the *arche* (cause), the *telos* (goal) and the activity of doing or deliberating are immanent to each other and immanent to the soul. *Praxis* is indeed, first and foremost, the energy, the immanent activity of the soul (*psyches energeia*). And I hasten to add that, in the context of the EN, *praxis* is fundamentally understood as *praxis teleia*: self-realising, self-finalised action.15 *Praxis* is human action as spiritual action: acting and in-acting according to excellence of virtue. It is acting fully, acting perfectly according to the teleological order of man's own being that is the *psyche*, the soul or mind. At EN, 1176b 5ff, Aristotle speaks of happiness as being self-sufficient (autarchic) and lacking in nothing; and of activities "*desirable in themselves which do not aim at any result beyond the mere exercise of the activity*".

> Happiness lacks nothing, and is self-sufficient. But those activities are desirable in themselves which do not aim at any result beyond the mere exercise of the activity. Now this is felt to be the nature of actions in conformity with virtue: for to do noble and virtuous deeds is a thing desirable for its own sake.

We know how, in the same Book X of EN, Aristotle finally identifies *praxis* and *theoria*, action and contemplative wisdom which is a totally immanent activity. Hence, while *praxis* has no end outside itself and *acts*, "energetically", from within itself (in this like *physis*, for after all *praxis* is the activity that qualifies the *psyche*, and the soul, in turn, is the nature, the *physis* of living beings); *techne* and *poiesis*, on the contrary, *work*, from without, extrinsically, according to a transitive type of activity which aims at producing artefacts outside the maker.

Aristotle's intentions can be seen more clearly if we consider the distinction between *techne/poiesis* and *physis*. In his *Physica*, 192b 10ff,

41

Aristotle announces that natural beings are those that *have within themselves a principle of motion and rest*. So, clearly and unambiguously *physis* is understood and spoken of as

> the principle and cause of motion and rest to those things, and those things only, in which she inheres as according to the same very constitution of the things and not accidentally or extrinsically.16

Against *natural beings*, that have within themselves the very principle and reason of their motion, growth and self-unfolding, we have *artificial beings*, made and manufactured things. Of these, Aristotle states: *none of them has within itself the principle of its own making* .[17] And he soon adds:

> Generally this principle resides in some external agent, as in the case of the house and its builder, and so with all hand-made things.

Unlike hand-made things, *physis* is, at once, its own origin and cause (*arche*), and its own goal and aim (*telos*). Nature is the self-unfolding processual activity, from itself to itself, which constitutes the being of natural/physical beings. *Physis* is the universal process that sustains and constitutes the manifold activities of natural beings: generation, nutrition, growth, movement, appetite, desire, change, self-preservation. It is the activity of self-production, of self-forth-bringing: out of itself, according to itself, toward itself. Natural beings generate or produce other natural beings. Nature, *physis*, produces itself. It produces motion (*kinesis*) according to oppositions, in the natural beings, while in itself it is free of oppositions. As immanent force and activity of self-unfolding, and as one of the fundamental ways in which being comes to the light of presence and abides in stable presence, *physis* is the activity of self-presenting, from itself aiming at itself.

Having established and clarified the difference obtaining between *techne/poiesis* and *praxis*, on the one hand, and between *techne/poiesis* and *physis*, on the other hand, we read in the *Physica*, 194a 22: *he techne mimeitai ten physin*. This is customarily translated as: *art imitates nature*.

With this statement, and in the light of what we have found so far, we can now attempt to interpret the precise meaning of *mimesis*. Let us remark, to begin, that Aristotle does not say that *he techne mimeitai ta physika onta*, i.e. natural beings, things that have in themselves the source of motion and rest. The philosopher states quite unambiguously that art imitates *nature* itself, i.e. the very same universal process of unfolding and self-unfolding from itself to itself, the very internal, immanent order and activity of natural things. But obviously, understood as such, and according to Aristotle, *physis* is not a *thing*, an *object*, nor a *complex of things or objects*: nature is not a given datum and a given, empirically observable object. *How, then, could it possibly be copied and imitated?*[18]

Having stated that *art mimesises nature*, Aristotle speaks of *physis* in the light of the final cause or *telos*. And in this light he suggests a first analogy between nature and art, between *physis* and *techne/poiesis*.

> *Physis* is the goal for the sake of which the rest exists, for if any systematic and continuous movement is directed to a goal, this goal is an end in the sense of the purpose to which the movement is a means (...) In the arts, too, it is in view of the end that the materials are either made or suitably prepared, and we make use of all things that we have at our command as though they existed for our sake; for we are, in a way, a goal ourselves.[19]

As natural processes are a goal to themselves, so artificial processes, emerging from an *eidos*, a mental plan, image and model, in man's soul/mind,[20] have man as their goal and aim.

This first analogy is further developed in *Physica*, 199a 8-19. Here Aristotle clearly suggests one of the meanings of the *mimetic* relationship obtaining between *techne/poiesis* and physis.

> Further, in any operation of human art, where there is an end to be achieved, the earlier and successive stages of the operation are performed for the purpose of realising that end. Now, when a thing is produced by nature, the earlier stages in every case lead up to the final development, in the same way as in the operation of art.(...) The operation, as well as the natural process, is directed and guided by a purpose. Thus, if a house were a natural product, the process would go through the same stages that it in fact undergoes when it is produced by art; and if natural products could also be produced by art, they would move along the same line that the natural process actually takes. (...) If, then, artificial processes are purposeful, so are natural processes too.

This passage establishes unequivocally the very strict parallelism, the closest analogy and what may be called the structural isomorphism obtaining between *techne/poiesis* and *physis*. The very same specular and circular formulation of the argument emphasises the analogy of the two processes: the natural and the technical/artistic.

In the light of the extensively quoted text from the *Physica*, I would suggest that we translate the sentence: *he techne mimeitai ten physin*, not as: *art imitates nature,* but rather in the following manner: *art produces by making extrinsically, as nature acts immanently.*[21] The artistic *making* is *mimetic* of nature, for it tends to proceed, towards a goal, according to the laws of the organic and ordered process which constitutes nature's *doing*: its self-unfolding towards its own goal. Art produces, extrinsically, according to the organic order of motion that aims at a purpose, and that originates from a disposition in the mind. Art, again, does not *imitate*, in the sense of *copying* or *portraying* nature; but simply proceeds, through making and not doing/acting, in view of a goal, starting from a disposition, a mental picture in the soul, and according to an ordered and organised process.

That *mimesis* does not mainly, primarily and exclusively mean copy and imitation should be seen more sharply in the light of the well known passage in the *Poetica,* 1451a 36ff, where Aristotle contrasts *poiesis* and *historia*, i.e. poetry and historiography.

> The poet's task is not to tell what has happened but the kind of things that can happen, i.e. the kind of events that are possible according to probability or necessity (...); the historian tells what has happened, the poet the kind of things that can happen. And in fact this is why the writing of poetry (*poiesis*) is a more philosophical activity, and one to be taken more seriously, than the writing of history; for poetry tells us rather the universals, historiography the particulars.

Although the word *mimesis* does not appear in this text, the quoted passage is nonetheless quite revealing. It tells us that the *content*, as it were, of poetry differs radically from that of historiography. The latter gathers and reconstructs past, given, occurred events, embedded as they are in the particularity of the particular occurrence, the particular context, the particular agent. Historiography presents us with facts, data, as objectively and minutely documented as possible: it reconstructs and interprets factual events. Poetry, on the contrary, gathers and grasps what could be according to probability and what ought to be according to necessity. Hence, it does not collate and refer stories about data from past events. It rather builds and projects the sequence, the meaning, the process of actions as they could and as they should be, according to necessary probabilities. In so far as the poet does not deal with given facts and events, with what has happened, with empirically given data, his specific activity of *mimesising* cannot be understood as the activity of *copying or representing*. This must be so, because the *object* of poetry: the possible, the probable, the necessary, what could be and what ought to be, *are not empirically given facts, data and phenomena!*[22]

Finally, *what* does the poet/artist *mimesise*? The poet is a poet by virtue of his *mimesis*, and the things he *mimesises* are *actions* (*praxeis*).[23] Once again, to translate *mimesis* as *imitation* would be, to say the least, misleading, superficial, distracting, indeed inadequate and incorrect. Poetry does not copy, imitate or mime actions: *it rather brings forth, it produces, it invents actions.* More precisely, it brings forth *mian praxin*: *one action*, totally and perfectly unified within itself. The reference to another text, in the *Poetica*, should help us clarify Aristotle's understanding of *praxis* as object of poetry, while absolving us from the more demanding task of providing a more comprehensive treatment of the problem.[24]

> A plot is not unified, as some people think, simply by having to do with one individual; for many things, in fact an infinite number, happen to an individual, some of which do not contribute to any unity; and in the same way there are many actions of a single individual, out of which no single action emerges. Hence it stands to reason that all those poets are wrong who have composed a Heracleid or a Theseid or poems of that kind. They think that since Heracles was a single individual, it naturally follows that the plot is also one. But Homer, superior as he is in other ways as well, seems to have seen this point in its proper light also, thanks either to art or to natural endowment. For in composing an Odyssey he did not incorporate into it everything that happened to the hero, for example how he was wounded on Parnassus, or how he pretended to go mad at the muster, neither of which events, by happening, made it necessary or probable for the other to happen; rather he constructed the Odyssey around *a single action* (*peri mian praxin*) of the kind we are talking about, and the Iliad in the same way.

This long passage should resolve the ambiguity, sometimes real, sometimes apparent, in Aristotle's employment of the words *praxis* and *praxeis*, in the singular and the plural form. It should also illumine the metaphysical meaning of *action*. Clearly, Aristotle is not referring to individual, isolated, accidental *actions* understood as *behaviour*: at least not primarily and not essentially. Nor is he solely thinking, in the context of the *Poetica*, of the dramatic action (or better plot) to be represented theatrically on stage. And when, as in the quoted passage, the plural form, *praxeis*, suggests the meaning of accidental, inconsequential, uneventful behaviouristic occurrence, Aristotle emphatically remarks that *poetry* even when given in the genre of a manifold and labyrinthine epic saga *mimesises one single action*: one single spiritual event, one single immanent order, one single mental project. For *praxis*, as I stated at the beginning, with reference to the *Nicomachean Ethics*, whose thematic theme is precisely *praxis*, is the unfolding of the immanent action/doing or activity of the soul/mind and of the soul/mind's immanent energy (*energeia*). Obviously, again, the internal operations or the immanent life of the soul/mind, *cannot be imitated nor can they be copied*!

Just as poetry proceeds by making-as-nature-does, so poetry proceeds by producing-as-the-psyche-acts. Furthermore, that poetry *mimeitai praxin* or mimesises action can be interpreted as meaning that poetry brings forth, manifests, presents and re-presents the essential activity of man's soul/mind. *Mimesis*, thus, is understood as the activity and the process of bringing forth or pro-ducing man's essential being, his *action* which is finally the unfolding of the energy or immanent activity of the soul.

In his Metaphysica, 1032b 1, Aristotle states:

> art produces those things whose model (*eidos*) and image reside in the soul.

Even that which proceeds from the *mimetic* activity of *techne/poiesis* has its *eidos* in man's soul. Hence, *mimesis* can produce the perfection of analogical syntheses, the revelation of universal truths, the revelation of the essence of man's being-in-action. In this light, by reinterpreting *mimesis* as manifestation of being and production of man's being, the Greek tragedy and epic poetry can be seen as the creative celebration of the human world ruled as it is, according to the Greek mind, by its immanent order, teleology and destiny.

The Originality of Plotinus' Aesthetics

The aesthetic experience is like an angel.
(Plotinus)

I want to commence this chapter by underlining a fundamental tenet of any responsible hermeneutical exercise. The idea that we can justifiably claim and be assured of an adequate understanding of the past and of past messages, distant by centuries from us and belonging to cultures quite different from our own; the idea, in other words, according to which we can engage in a fruitful ever-present and ever-living dialogue with the voices of our ancestors because we fundamentally belong to the same *tradition,* can also be aptly formulated in the terms of the rhetorical questions: "How do we recognise a messenger of novelty? Is not our disposition to understand what is *new* necessarily predetermined by the *old* in which we are immersed?"[1]

The same tenet and precept of hermeneutical discourse could be rendered otherwise and, hence, perhaps extended in its meaning and significance. If it is true that even in the increasingly accelerated progress of technology, new discoveries neither substitute nor render obsolete previous achievements, no matter how elementary, primitive and unsophisticated they may be, so that, for instance, we still need and employ fire, round wheels, knives to cut bread, sandals to walk safely, simple but perfectly efficient tools to till the land...; if this is true of technology, it is just as true of the history of our ideas of reality, the world, ourselves, the gods, art and beauty.[2]

In my dialogue with past philosophers, I find the revisitation of Plotinus particularly rewarding. In what follows I shall attempt to suggest some of the reasons why this is so for me, by focussing on Plotinus' meditations on beauty and art, elegantly inset as they are in one of the most elegant, inspiring and lyrical systems of philosophy.

Contemporary philosophical reflection has, by and large, abandoned the Platonically motivated aesthetic ambition at formulating theories of beauty, in favour of poetic investigations aiming at qualifying and refining the

47

concept of art as a process of production and a practical modality and, hence, the structural, linguistic, formal make-up of aesthetic artefacts.[3] We may safely say that aesthetics has given way to poetics, the philosophy of beauty has been replaced by the philosophy of art, Aristotle is in fashion somewhat at the expense of Plato, ontological models grounded on the principle of transcendence have been discarded in favour of anthropological immanence and the indwelling of subjectivity in language or, at the extreme, historical and existential facticity and the penultimate void of pre-structured absence.

In extremis, the recently past so-called postmodern and deconstructive gestures and experiments, in their suspicious mistrust of order, speculative rationality, logical coherence and no matter how asymptotic attempts at inclusive explanatory or heuristic models, betray the propensity towards fragmentation, ephemeral curiosity, superficiality and the inability to think clearly and seriously of art and of philosophy.[4]

Equally alarming and symptomatic are the cries of the *death of Art* and the *death of beauty* that hailed the inception of our century and guided avant-garde poetics to the point of silence or endless inescapable experimentation.[5] Interestingly, and fortunately, the generally prevailing and fashionable anti-beauty and anti-system critical, poetic and philosophical stances do not provide a substitute for our irrepressible need to find in art the epiphanic celebration of an ideal order of world and experience, the perfect correspondence between what is manifested and how it is manifested, the intuitive and immediate experience of being *arrested* in a moment of qualitative absoluteness.[6]

The Third century of the Christian era was the veritable end of the beginning of Western culture, born on Greek shores, then disseminated, preserved and mediated by the Roman Empire and, even earlier and for a longer time, by the Hellenistic *koiné* with Alexandria as one of its most sophisticated gravitational centres. If the end of a beginning, however, the third century was also the beginning of an end: that of the apogee of the *pax romana*, with the first sign of stress and strain in an edifice too large and too diversified to be held together even by the unsurpassed engineering talent of the imperial Romans, masterbuilders of politics, law and administration. Rome, initially *colonised* by the refining artistic and intellectual influence of fading Athens, is, in the century of Plotinus, spiritually nourished by Egypt, where the elegant and rational spirit of Greece (much indebted, anyway, to ancient Egypt) symbiotically merged with Oriental intuition, mysticism and theology, not to mention the rising spirit of the new religion. With its deeply rooted and long lasting tradition, Egypt, more so than any other ancient culture, could best absorb, assimilate, filter and revitalise those different and manifold forces, to produce yet another golden era in its history, yet another *renaissance* in its culture, marked by sophisticated subtlety, vigour and originality.

Plotinus is among numerous others, the greatest and most eloquent exponent of Egyptian culture and of Western culture in the third century. His *Enneades,* a profound and thoughtful work of maturity, is in many respects one of the most distinct documents of philosophical wisdom. More so, beyond its obvious analogies with and references to other philosophies, beyond its informative intertextual merits, this is quite a singular work. Let us first note that Plotinus, as father of Neo-platonism, has deeply influenced Christianity, its theology and philosophy. Augustine, Pseudo-Dionysius and, hence, Scotus Eriugena and later Thomas Aquinas, to mention but a few in particular; more generally, the entire Patristic and Scholastic tradition, are all deeply indebted to the philosopher from Lycopolis. We must acknowledge, in other words, that Plotinus's philosophy is the meeting point of Greece and Rome, East and West, Ancient Egypt and the new world, pagan mysteries and the Christian faith.[7]

The entire philosophy of Plotinus is inspired and sustained by an all-pervasive search for unity in all things: it is the sublime celebration of an ordered and harmonious universe.[8] The reflection upon our human experience, epistemic, psychological, affective, moral, aesthetic, with its characteristic teleological dynamism, on the one hand, and, on the other hand, the ontological requirements to establish a beginning capable of accounting, at once, for unity and diversity, singularity and plurality, totality and particularity, harmony and dissonance, light and darkness, perfection and imperfection, system and fragments, speculatively justify Plotinus' beginning from the beginning conceived of as self-sufficient Unity, the One: the supreme affirmation of being, the highest hypostatic order.

The One is the primordial source of all reality as much as the final goal to which all reality aspires. The manifold plurality of distinct beings emanates from the self-effusive fulness of the One; it is *produced* by the participated super-abundance of the most perfect One, only to return to the One as to its source and goal, there to find its rest, fulfilment and final verification or truth. The sun cannot but diffuse the rays of its light. And we as the pilgrim rays of the One, cannot find rest in the element of multiplicity, dispersion and fragmentation. We carry within ourselves the deep nostalgia for infinity and perfect unity and harmony: because we are that very nostalgia. Unity and infinity are already within us, urging our thought inevitably immersed in the realm of distinctions, to go beyond the bounds of what is thinkable. The One is the effusive source of multiplicity, and our soul, dissatisfied with the limitations, the imperfections, the metaphysical insufficiency of multiplicity, though unable to know (as we know) and utter (as we speak) the perfections of Unity, holds of it an intuitive, religious and mystical, inner vision. Unknowable and unspeakable, but by being known and uttered for what it is not, the One is nonetheless present to our mind. Our experience of communion with the mystery of the Infinite, Good, Archetypal One (which transcends all categorisation and from which we ontologically depend) is an act of recognition of that mystery, and presupposes an intuitive disposition, a spiritual attunement, a connatural *sympathy*. The One, as the First and hence as metaphysical foundation, does not however inertly abide in total solitude: it is not an *abstract* unity and identity. Rather, in self-effusion of inexhaustible perfection, it *generates* or posits its first opposition, its *other,* the Intellect: the *Nous*. As Plotinus puts it, in a lapidary expression pregnant of original meaning: *if you suppress otherness, you will have only indistinct unity, silent.*[9] As the first generated hypostasis, the *Nous* constitutes the first event of diversity and differentiation, otherness and relatedness. Dialectically, we can safely say, a *relative opposition* unites the One and the eternal Intellect. One is for the Other, and vice-versa. One is in function of the Other, and vice-versa. In its eternal contemplation of the One, in purely spiritual vision or *theoria* , the *Nous* thinks the totality of all eternal ideas and essences. Similar to the One, the intellect beholds in perfect unity and harmony the multiplicity of all purely intelligible ideas. Plotinus can, hence, call the *Nous: one-all*. The *Nous,* furthermore, acts as an inward silent poet and craftsman.

If the *Nous,* dependent from the One, explains the intelligibility of Being, Unity-in-diversity and the ideas, Plotinus conceives a needed third hypostasis: the Soul as the intermediary link *(metaxú)* and meeting point between intelligible ideas and empirical sensuous reality. In silent and fertile contemplation of the *Nous,* the Soul, as unconscious and extrovert poetic power, generates the lower realm of sensations and of sensibilia, being at once the principle of life and generation, in time.[10] Farther removed from the One, and more closely related to multiplicity, the Soul is the synthesis of eternal ideas and ephemeral sense-perceptions. It is eternal, yet in time. Eternally contemplating the eternal *Nous* that makes her pregnant with perfection of unity, the Soul generates, in time, the cosmic *anima mundi* and, more diversified, the individual souls of individual living beings united only according to their genus and species. One and eternal, the soul generates a multiplicity of living souls. It is, hence, called one-and-many. With the birth of the *anima mundi,* time is born, cyclically and harmoniously held together, in its fragmented events, by the unifying force of the Soul from which all things visible, tangible and perceptible proceed and which holds all things in perennial life, order, harmony, beauty. Everything, immersed as it is in the emanated flux (*aporroia*) of participated perfection, brings within itself the mark of its unitary origin and the nostalgia to return to perfect one-ness. Everything is organically linked to the life of the whole and therefore is the sign (*semeion*), symbol and messenger of everything else.

Beyond and below the three unitary hypostases: the One, the Intellect, the Soul; lies the empty, boundless, indetermined simplicity of matter as obscure non-being: pure privation, powerless, naked potentiality, pure possibility to be. Nothing in itself, it can be informed by the soul and hence give rise to the world of contingent, unstable, diversified, ephemeral appearances: the fragmentation of the intelligible Archytype into the physical multiplicity of sense-experience. "Ashamed of being in the body", embarrassed by its proximity to matter, while at once intuitively contemplating the order of the universe in the *anima mundi,* the eternal Soul, the Intellect, the supreme One; the human soul, a wonderful *amphibian!*[11], is the true central *protagonist(protos agonistes)* of the Plotinian universe.

In its living activity, the soul is the concrete synthesis of time and eternity, unity and diversity, intelligibility and perception, ontological perfection and empirical deficiency. Dramatically distracted in its composite and symbiotic nature, the soul aspires to rest in perfect unity, it strives to divest itself of the transitory illusions of empirical experience. It desires eternal unity with its adequate object of knowledge and love, from which it originally proceeded. Through spiritual, philosophical, cultural, moral and aesthetic refinement the soul attunes itself to Truth, Goodness, Beauty, thus making itself ready for the unspeakable contemplation of the One.[12] The soul's spiritual purification must, finally, be guided by rational thought (that *knows how* to see, to love, to act ethically) without which art, love, virtue, would be blind and remain lost and entangled in a web of insufficient, imperfect, material goals and aims. I must stress, however, that with the central role absolved by the Soul/soul, as protagonist of a metaphysical adventure at once transcendent and immanent, Plotinus has produced a rewarding synthesis, and a veritable enrichment, of Platonic and Aristotelian principles: a synthesis of transcendence and immanence, metaphysics and psychology, epistemology, ethics, aesthetics. I must also express my conviction that, in the case of Plotinus, we are confronted with the first scientific attempt, in Western thought, at an organic and wholistic *system.*[13] The metaphysical hypostases are, if not *transcendentally deduced* as in Kant and Hegel, produced, projected and posited after observation of imperfect experience and, hence, after induction. In this Plotinus pays his partial debt to Aristotle.

With reference to the purely speculative and logical character of Plotinus' system, I confess my sense of gratification with the idea of *divine aporroia:* the principle of *emanation* as the force and breath of the Plotinian universe. With the all-pervasive principle of emanation, the perennial movement of expansion and retention, ebb and flow of being, the journey from One to many and from multiplicity to One-ness again, from light to darkness and back to light again, Plotinus has produced an organic and dynamic system that (though not *transcendentally deduced,* as is noted by most critics, but intuitively and inductively *invented)* overcomes the limitations and forced restraints of the more *categorised* and *essentialist* Christian world-view, with its distinctions and separation between God, free and transcendent, and the world.[14]

In the light of what preceded, a few remarks (brief and simplifying) again, must be made about some aesthetic and poetic intuitions in Plotinus's doctrine, in order to underline the wisdom and originality of this philosopher. It is quite obvious that, apart from its internal aesthetic merit and elegance, apart from the exquisitely lyrical diction of Plotinus, the dynamic, organic, ordered and synthetic system of this luminary thinker from Lycopolis and Alexandria, was so construed that it could eminently enlighten the essence and nature of art and beauty. Plotinus's aesthetics is universally acknowledged to be quite original; because sustained by a very original philosophical system, I hasten to add. It represents the synthesis of Hellenic and Hellenistic reflections on the questions, problems, wonderful and mysterious alchemy of art and beauty. It is a general, global and foundational theory; again contained within a wholistic system. It is "new both in its metaphysical foundations and in its empirical analyses of beauty".[15] Unlike Plato, and more like Aristotle, though thematically more explicit than Aristotle himself, Plotinus "highly appreciated sensory beauty" which is the most perfect property and, indeed, the only true perfect property of the sensory world, for sensory beauty carries within itself the mark of perfect unity and intelligibilty. Plotinus' aesthetics, as indeed his entire system, overcomes the bounds of dualistic models: even in this much closer to Aristotle than to Plato. Furthermore, without sacrificing or ignoring the needs of an empirically and critically grounded discourse on poetics and art, Plotinus articulates a metaphysical foundation and justification of beauty. By thus reconciling and synthesising the Platonic and Aristotelian approaches to art and beauty, Plotinus proves his erudition, the speculative merit of his intuitions and his creative originality. In his critical rejection of the naive and traditional criteria of beauty, originally thematised by the mathematical Pythagoreans, namely the criteria of symmetry and proportion, Plotinus implicitly articulates a critique of naive naturalism, while at once stressing the metaphysical character and function of beauty and of art. By suggesting that beauty consists rather in a more fundamental *quality* that shines through and at once sustains symmetry and proportion, Plotinus frees aesthetics from the overtones of Platonic mythology and sets it on the course on scientific investigation. In focussing on the qualitative nature of beauty and art, Plotinus is the veritable father and forerunner of modern aesthetics. Equally significant is his critique of yet another uncritically and superficially adopted criterion of art and beauty, namely the criterion of *mimesis,* with its naively naturalistic connotations. Though not explicitly acknowledged, Plotinus's critique of *mimesis* constitutes, to my mind, an echo and a more perceptive revisitation of Aristotle's conception of *imitation.*[16] Finally, having overcome the naturalistic, quantitative, dualistic, naively mimetic conceptions of art and beauty, Plotinus, first in the history of Western thought, thematised the indissoluble interaction and symbiosis of art and beauty. Thus, for the first time, it is clearly established that art belongs to the realm of beauty and that beauty belongs essentially to the realm of art. Sensory beauty is the result and outcome of artistic procedures: the synthetic activity of the soul and the creative *protagonist* of the Plotinian universe. Even in this, we are indebted to the Egyptian philosopher. Furthermore, apart from his original reformulation, improvement and expansion of past models of reflection on art and beauty and of past modes of sensibility,[17] Plotinus stands for us as the beacon of comforting light and inspiration in our distracted, dissipated, mercantile, at times and often superficial and decorative postmodern culture. If Rome, and later the middle ages and the Renaissance, Hegel and Bergson, could be enriched by the teaching of Plotinus; our contemporary culture, not unlike that of Third Century Rome: at the end of a beginning and at a beginning of an end, can equally be nourished by the wise, tolerant, cosmopolitan philosopher from Lycopolis and Alexandria who emigrated to the centre of disintegration in order to disseminate his seeds of reintegration.

Hegel's Aesthetics and *the End of Art*

In art we are dealing with an unfolding of truth

Diogenes Laertius reports that: "When someone inquired why we spend much time conversing about beautiful things", Aristotle answered by saying: "This is the question of a blind man". It would equally be a blind man's question to ask why Hegel found it possible, indeed necessary to treat the subject of art scientifically and systematically. Hegel's speculative system is the fruit of a philosophical culture based on the supremacy and centrality of the rational subject. The world of subjectivity was born with the Copernican revolutions, the transoceanic journeys, the new scientific conquests, the Protestant Reformation, the Cartesian ego-centred foundation. In this *brave new world* all the expressions of the human subject become the unique and central object of reflection. Hegel does not tire of stressing this point:

> The Universal and absolute need from which art (on its formal side) springs, has its origin in the fact that man is a thinking consciousness, i.e. that man draws out of himself and puts before himself what he is and whatever else he is.1

All the well-known motifs of the past and of tradition are found in Hegel's definition of art and artistic beauty. Beauty is qualified as symmetry, order, proportion, harmony, splendour, synthesis of spirit and tangible matter, synthesis of knowledge and delight, unity of opposites, tangible manifestation and incarnation of spiritual forms. More specifically: *In art we are dealing with an unfolding of truth*. This is the often repeated and variously orchestrated *Leitmotiv* and refrain of Hegel's *Aesthetik*. Artistic beauty is, thus, understood as a supreme form of absolute truth. And the *Aesthetik* constitutes the last and most elaborate theodicy of art and of artistic beauty.

Truth, according to Hegel, is the synthesis of opposites or the synthesis of the real and the ideal. It is the result of the process through which the *concept* (as abstract, potential reality in the embryonic state of *seed)* is concretised, objectivised and alienated, eventually reaching its substantial fullness, its achievement as *idea*. Art, in so far as it is a form of the self-revelation of truth: tangible truth, is itself conciliation and synthesis. In art and in the works of art a synthesis is realised between *a content and the way in which it is manifested,* a synthesis of content and form. Art is the synthesis of an abstract universal content, and a particular tangible form. In a word, it is the synthesis of spiritual images and of tangible material appearance. In such a synthesis, the tangible exists and is given *for* the mind. On the other hand, the spiritual element is given in the tangible. *The work of art stands between the immediately tangible and ideal thought.* Again, to rephrase, *the tangible in art is spiritualised since the spiritual appears in it as tangible.*

The real *crux* for idealism, as for philosophy as such, is the difference between spirit and nature, man and the world, essence and life.2 This division and separation is bridged and healed by beauty which is precisely the compenetration of the universal and the particular, of the end and the means, of the concept and the object. Art manifests the idea in the tangible. The imagination *produces* sense-perceivable images of ideas. And the ideas, the spiritual contents expressed physically in works of art, are called *the deep and universal human interests, the most ample truths of the spirit, the universal powers that govern in every era:*

> In their works of art the nations have deposited their richest inner intuitions and ideas, and art is often the key, and in many nations the sole key, to understanding their philosophy and religion.3

The contents of art are moments in which the mind reveals itself and becomes conscious of itself, through its history. They represent the epochal visions and the profound modes of conceiving reality in different cultures. They are different moments of truth: the different modes through which reality reaches the light of human consciousness along its historical development. History itself is precisely history of thought and of truth. Seen in its completion, at the end as it were of its Odyssey, history is also called *idea* or *spirit*. And these are also called, by Hegel, *reason:* which is divine reason thinking-loving itself in the human reason, and vice-versa. The absolute is, finally, the infinitely free and infinitely necessary synthesis of man and God.

Art is the expression of truth in a tangible, sense-perceptible manner. A particular conception of the world and of reality in general, and a particular stage of absolute truth, is at work, as an epochal presupposition, a

Volksgeist and *Weltzustand,* a universal pre-disposition and a categorical way of addressing reality, in each particular age, epoch, culture or civilisation. From this follows Hegel's distinction among art-epochs.[4] Symbolic art, pre-Greek, especially Egyptian and Oriental art, *seeks* adequacy between an idea of the absolute which is all too abstract and under-developed, and the tangible world of its physical expressions. The anxiously sought-after adequacy is never realised in symbolic art. Classical, that is Greek, art discovers and *embodies* this adequacy between an anthropomorphic idea of the spirit (the Greek gods) and an anthropomorphic tangible or physical element (the human body). On the other hand, Christian and Romantic[5] art gives expression to an idea of the absolute which, because of its highly developed form, cannot be adequately and harmoniously contained and embodied in physical apparitions. Art-forms disintegrate. The classical harmony is disrupted.[6] The fulfilment of man's spiritual needs once attained in and through art, is now to be sought and to be found only in reflection: *Thinking and reflection have superseded fine art.*

Hegel never intended to deny the existence of individual artists both in his and in future times; much less did he believe the *end of art* to be a *fait accompli* and a total death, as it were, which would have wiped art from the face of the earth.[7] Let us read the last paragraph of the Introduction to the *Aesthetik:*

> Now, therefore, what the particular arts realise in individual works of art is, according to the Concept of art, only the universal forms of the self-unfolding Idea of beauty. It is as the external actualisation of this Idea that the wide Pantheon of art is rising. Its architect and builder is the self-comprehending spirit of beauty, but to complete it will need the history of the world and its development through thousands of years.[8]

In the entire development of the history of the world there will be art. Art however, after the foundation of subjective philosophy and after Idealism, will no longer represent a universal, adequate and sufficient mode of grasping the absolute as such or indeed of satisfying the essential needs of the human mind.

The transition from the classical to the modern world was marked by the discovery of self-conscious and self-justifying subjectivity. With this, the concept of reality as stable substance only, was simultaneously repudiated and transcended. The universal predisposition of man in the classical world to rely on the imaginative and mytho-poetic faculty[9] changes, in the modern world, into a reliance on reason, reflection, scientific experimental exploration and analytical observation. Hegel could observe with historical correctness:

> ...it is certainly the case that art no longer affords the satisfaction of spiritual needs which earlier ages and nations sought in it and found in it alone...The beautiful days of Greek art, like the golden age of the Middle Ages are gone.10

Art is something of the past, Hegel adds.

It would be premature, at this point, to attempt a global appraisal of the correctness of Hegel's intuition. On the other hand it does not seem premature to express some doubts and to ask, in the light of Hegel's statements: is it after all true that the Greek, Medieval and Renaissance conceptions of the world fostered and produced a splendid artistic growth as a well-nourished tree spontaneously produces abundant foliage? Is it really true that those peoples and civilisations were more artistic than we moderns? Finally, is it true that the modern world is more *philosophic* than the ancient world?

Hegel conceived art to be an absolute form of the spirit, a universal phenomenon and a necessitating epochal force: a mode of being and thinking that characterises and determines in a fundamental and prereflective manner particular moments in the history of mankind. Thus understood, as a constitutive force of an epoch, as the substantial form of an epoch, art no longer is. For us moderns art is something of the past. Art does not represent any longer the way or form in which we affirm the truth, the way in which we become conscious of reality, of ourselves and of God, the way in which we interpret, we constitute and project the meaning of our world. Art is no longer the *topos* in which the total image of our world is reflected and brought to consciousness. Therefore, art is no longer the *topos* of truth:

> ...there is a deeper comprehension of truth which is no longer so akin and friendly to sense as to be capable of appropriate adoption and expression in this medium. The Christian view of truth is of this kind and, above all, the spirit of our world today, or more particularly, of our religion and the development of our reason, appears as beyond the stage at which art is the supreme mode of our knowledge of the absolute.11

Hegel adds immediately: *Thought and reflection have gone beyond, have superseded fine art.*12

The motifs of the *passing away* of art, which appear right from the start of the *Aesthetik,* are constantly repeated throughout the work. Hegel repeats the logical and theoritical motifs already mentioned, when he treats of the relationship obtaining between art, religion and philosophy. Here we find a more explicit treatment of the relation between the history of thought and the position of art within the context of the human knowledge of the absolute:

> Thus, for example, in the case of the Greeks, art was the highest form in which the people represented the gods to themselves and gave themselves some awareness of truth...
>
> In general it was early in history that thought passed judgement against art as a mode of illustrating the idea of the Divine;...and indeed even with the Greeks, for Plato opposed the Gods of Homer and Hesiod starkly enough.
>
> With the advance of civilisation a time comes in the case of every people when art points beyond itself...When the urge for knowledge and research, and the need for inner spirituality instigated the Reformation, religious ideas were drawn away from their wrapping in the element of sense and brought back to the inwardness of heart and thinking. Thus the *after* of art consists in the fact that there dwells in the spirit the need to satisfy itself solely in its own inner self as the true form of truth to take.[13]

The last sentence, in which Hegel underlines the process of interiorisation as characteristic of the post-reformation culture, could be read as a *manifesto* of Romanticism.

The historian and literary critic, Erich Heller, in his significant and eloquent work *The Artist's Journey into the Interior,* analyses and compares the motifs of arts's crisis in Hegel's *Aesthetik* and the process of interiorisation unfolding in the Romantic consciousness. Heller shows how at the end of the Romantic experience the world is conceived, constituted and experienced as *inwardness: Nowhere will be world but within.* There will be no other reality but that which is edified in the innermost chambers of the soul, and separated from the outer world as from a non-reality. In the same study, Heller dealing with the problem of Realism, understood as the heritage and result of the Romantic crisis, reaches the same conclusion: "External reality has no claims any more to being real. The only real world is the world of human inwardness".[14] Another enlightening aspect of Heller's perspicacious analysis is discovered in a reference to the poet T.S. Eliot seen as a critic of Shakespeare. In his essay, *Hamlet and his Problem,* Eliot shows how the work is a tragedy *manquée,* a work that pre-announces, and already suffers from, the Romantic crisis. Hamlet is a solitary subject, divided, removed and estranged from the world.[15] His personality, the character, permits neither an encounter nor a confrontation with reality. Hamlet lives totally within the bounds of the soul's inner life; deprived and free of any form of natural, historical, objective constriction. An interior character, existential *ante litteram,* like Hamlet, totally estranged from the world, causes the tragedy to become an artistic failure because the hero's emotion goes beyond the concrete situation. So Eliot denounces what he calls the lack of *objective correlative*. He notes a chasm, a lack of correlation between the soul and the world. Hamlet's soul is totally separated from reality. The world has in his eyes no existence. In this respect Hamlet is a prototype of Romantic consciousness.

Romantic art finds itself in a contradictory situation. Delighting in interiority and faced with the problem of otherness, it generates the *impossible synthesis*. Eliot's denunciation of modernism as born from the *dissociation of sensibility*[16], the dissociation of sensibility from the intellect, shows that what is at stake is the whole of Romantic and post-Romantic art. To return to Hegel, I feel justified in attributing to him the merit of foreseeing what the entire legion of literary critics have, since, written about Romanticism. There is nothing discussed in its critical literature, that cannot be found in Hegel's *Aesthetik*. What the philosopher liked to call *the prose of life* indicates not only the experience or writing *grey upon grey* the conceptual journals of the mind philosophically mature. Even more, it points to the experience of division and estrangement of the soul. Would the natural consequence of this then be the loss of the very concept of artistic beauty or of the unity of mind and reality, spirit and matter, image and form? Hegel says in pregnant terms of Romantic art:

> The inner world constitutes the content of the Romantic sphere and must therefore be represented as this inwardness and in the pure appearance of this depth of feeling. Inwardness celebrates its triumph over the external and manifests its victory in and on the external itself, whereby what is apparent to the senses alone sinks into worthlessness,...
>   Thereby the separation of idea and shape, their indifference and inadequacy to each other, come to the fore again, as in symbolic art,...
>   This we take to be the general character of the symbolic, classical and romantic forms of art, as the three relations of the idea to this shape in the sphere of art. They consist in the striving for, the attainment, and the transcendence of the Ideal as the true Idea of beauty.[17]

If we want to attempt some provisional conclusions, we ought to note that Romantic art, as appraised by Hegel, is much less than symbolic art. If art is the *topos* of the synthesis of mind and world, Romantic art, which attempts to *destroy the external world,* in the long run denies the very conditions for the possibility of that synthesis. By going beyond that ideal synthesis, Romantic art moves away from the true idea of beauty. Romantic art is already an *anti-art*. With Romanticism we are well on the way to modernism and all forms of abstractionism in art.

We are aware that all avant-garde movements have originated as protests against the dogmatically stated, extreme solutions of their predecessors, particularly of the Romantics; that the crisis of beauty, of the synthetic union of spirit and nature in art, has its causes in the very roots of the modern world. Let us, therefore, comment on a host of problems that pre-occupied Hegel from his youth. The mention of these preoccupations will help us to appraise more concretely Hegel's concept of truth and of truth in art. Moreover, it will introduce some new elements, for instance the relationship between art and society. From his youth, as a result of his quite abundant reading in art-history and of his keen interest in Greek civilisation, Hegel had intuited that a great art, whose works adequately signify the synthesis of epochal thought, is possible only in a fully developed culture and in a harmoniously organised society in which individual and collective interests were reconciled.[18] J. Taminiaux aptly remarks: "Before Marx, the young Hegel affirms that not only art expresses a civilisation, but furthermore that a great art is impossible in a divided society."[19]

A unified and organic culture would be such that its spiritual identity, its image, would be easily recognised in its traditions and, consequently, would be spontaneously *representable* artistically in its essential aspects.[20] It would be a society in which the relation between man, his gods and nature could find expression, through artistic imagination, without deviations, distractions, ulterior motives, and without intellectual distinctions and cerebral justifications.[21] Such a society, Hegel constantly suggests, and mentioned for the first time at the age of eighteen, was Greek society. In contrast, indeed in opposition to it, Hegel saw that his contemporary society was torn by conflicts between particular interests and collective ideals incapable of forging unity. Germany was not yet born! Germany and Europe, at the time, instead of presenting a clearly identifiable spiritual physiognomy, expressive of the essential aspects of the contemporary culture, exhibited the very opposite features. What was evident was the heterogeneous and divided panorama of a rather large number of traditions and cultural streams. This situation made it difficult, if not impossible, for the artist to render artistically, to give aesthetic form to the innumerable, contrasting, corrupt and forgotten or absent traditions. Just as artistic creation in a divided society is an almost impossible undertaking, the appreciation of beauty suffers a similar fate. Hegel, the eighteen-year old, had already intuited the dialectical relation obtaining between society, the individual and art.[22] The individual lives within and in dependence of his community. The rifts and divisions of society are also to be found in the individuals that make up society. They suffer, as the elder Hegel put it, the drama of the *unhappy consciousness*. The appreciation of art as well as creative artistic work become impossible in a similar societal state. In the context of a divided society we are again confronted with the situation of the Romantic consciousness and its pejorative form: *ironic consciousness*. The aesthetic solution is, then, found in the solitary and finally solipsistic experience of poetising on poetry. This is, to quote F. Schlegel, the hour of *the poetry of poetry*. Another passage from Hegel is also worth quoting:

> ...the vanity of everything factual, moral, and of intrinsic worth, the nullity of everything objective and absolutely valid. If the ego remains at this standpoint, everything appears to it as null and vain, except its own subjectivity which therefore becomes empty and hollow and itself mere vanity.23

This splendid page portrays the artist's soul in any epoch of cultural disorientation. We ought to underline the urgency and actuality of this psychological analysis, based as it is on a concrete historical experience and presupposing an integral phenomenology of consciousness in search of harmony with the world.24 The entire nihilistic consciousness and, in many respects, the existentialist consciousness correspond literally to this psychopathological analysis.

If art appeals to unity and presupposes it, art must be in close connection with truth which is unity. Greece, in the eyes of Hegel, was *true* in all its expression. The modern world is, for Hegel, false from head to toe. In Greek culture we rediscover the unity of a spontaneously expressible reality. The modern world provides false, accidental, one-sided and extremist expressions. In the Greek world we are, as in the Medieval and Renaissance worlds, in the presence of true art. In our culture we are surrounded by an infinity of fragmented expressions. These appear to be the convictions of the young Hegel. In the writings of the mature philosopher we find them *raised (Aufgehoben)* and absorbed into the logical architecture of a speculative system that, in the end, attenuates if not completely ignores the evidence of the earlier acute intuitions. One could undermine and totally deny the validity of those intuitions, by suggesting that they were totally grounded on the Romantic preconceived disposition to favour the cult of Greek civilisation. These prejudices, some critics and historians would argue, are the sole reason for Hegel's praise of Greek art and his criticism of the modern world. Similar arguments, to my mind, may well be convenient. They certainly do injustice to the complexity of the problem and to the complex articulation with which Hegel treated it. It seems that all too often and in a too facile manner, art-critics and aestheticians invoke the Romantic ascendancy as the reason for undermining and discarding the possible evidence which may lead to questioning the value of modern art and the possible meaning of the *end of art*.

Having traced some probable reasons and meanings of Hegel's argument that *art is something of the the past,* I should now announce further and perhaps more satisfactory interpretations. It is quite obvious that *meaning (Bedeutung)* and *content (Gehalt)* constitute the main preoccupation of Hegel's reflections on art. The crisis of Romantic art, indeed the *death of art,* is ascribed precisely to the fact that the artist removes himself from the ideal *contents;* ignores, reduces or vilifies them by immersing them in the *prose of life.* On the one hand, with Romanticism, "fools, louts, all sorts of everyday vulgarities, taverns, carters, chamber-pots and fleas"25 make their appearance on the stage of art; on the other hand, "the latest poetry has screwed itself up to endless fantasticalness and mendacity which is supposed to make an effect by its bizarre character, but it meets with no response in any sound heart, because in such refinements of reflection on what is true in human life, *every genuine content is evaporated.*" 6

I would suggest the hypothesis that, employing the language of semiology, Hegel understood the works of art or art-signs primarily as iconic signs, i.e. as signifiers of objective referents and denotata: facts or images, events, situations, *Volksgeist* and *Weltzustand.* He stated quite clearly:

> Indeed any word hints at a *meaning (Bedeutung)* and counts for nothing in itself. Similarly the spirit and the soul shine through the human eye, through a man's face, flesh, skin, through his whole figure, and here the *meaning* is always something wider than what shows itself in the immediate appearance. It is in this way that the work of art is to be *significant (bedeutend)* and not appear exhausted by these lines, curves, notes, word-sounds, or whatever other material is used; on the contrary, it should disclose an inner life, feeling, soul, a *content (Gehalt)* and spirit, which is just what we call the *significance (Bedeutung)* of a work of art.27

Consequently, Romantic art, in which *every genuine content is evaporated,* represents the end of iconographic and iconic art and,therefore, the death of art as Hegel conceived and knew it. It represents the end of a particular form of art.28

It is quite obvious, and ostensibly stated, that Hegel foresaw the future existence of a technically *more perfected,* formally more refined art. The fact, nonetheless, that the philosopher could announce the theme of the death of art, clearly suggests that he could understand art only in the light of its referential nature: in its mimetic, representative, *realistic* character and function. This should neither surprise nor irritate us. After all, Hegel was thinking of classical art which strongly foregrounds the referential nature of signs, because born of an ontological and onto-centered conception of the world. We could say, consequently, that Hegel was, in his understanding of art, a realist! I intended to suggest precisely this, when I stated that "the *Aesthetik* constitutes the last and most elaborate theodicy of art and artistic beauty". On the other hand Hegel holds most consequentially the *Idealistic* stance in his understanding and practice of logic and of philosophy, and in his conviction that art is finally resolved into philosophy.

The greatness of great art was shown to Hegel in classical art, the art of the past. Consequently, too, he was bound to foresee the final resolution of that art (an *objective* art, carrier of historical and ideal contents or meanings, and unfolding of truth) into and by subjective philosophy. Art is, in the end, resolved and transformed into aesthetics. Today we can translate the key-word of Hegel's aesthetics, namely the concept of *Erscheinung,* into the word/concept of *sign.* We are also granted, in a becoming world of probabilities, in a world that has tempered the dimensions of the psychic, reflective, projectual, inward subjectivity, the privilege to conceive systematically artistic signs as *signs of themselves.*

Hegel understood art, as expression of the past, complete, realised, *given* worlds (as totality), in the light of and from the view-point of signified contents. We think of art and make art in the light and from the view-point of the signifier's form and of the formal sign-making process.[29] Even in this we are indebted to Hegel.

Doktor Faustus' Mentor: Adorno and the Death of Art

*The fathers were in the desert, but the
desert was not in them: and this is music.*
(Kafka)

As an illustration and a development of some aspects of Hegel's questions concerning the *End of Art,* I shall analyse in this chapter the central themes of Adorno's philosophy of music. In particular Adorno can be rightly considered as the most faithfully unfaithful, and unfaithfully faithful of all the Hegelian disciples and followers. The analogy and par-allelism between Plato and Aristotle, on the one hand, and Hegel and Adorno, on the other hand, has often come to mind. If nothing else, the wonderful *simile* coined by Plato to qualify Aristotle's attitude towards his mentor, would perfectly apply to Adorno's disposition towards Hegel: "Like a frisky rebellious colt who kicks back at his mother". As we will see, in his aesthetic discourse, Adorno remains very close to Hegel's design. In his analysis of avant-garde, art, and music in particular, Adorno elaborates central concepts of Hegel's aesthetics.

In order to somewhat clarify my presentation, I will have to explore, intertextually, the interface between Adorno's philosophical thesis and the narrative world of Thomas Mann, especially the monumental and quite wonderful novel, *Dr Faustus.* If the message encoded in the novel and in Adorno's aesthetic theory will sound too pessimistic and extreme, let us take it as a healthy provocative reminder rather than a conclusive and complete explanation.

The very announcement of our theme: death of art, may sound a provocative attempt to revive old-fashioned nihilistic rancours. Furthermore, the theme should put us in the embarrassing position of somebody who seems to close his eyes and to disregard the existence of numerous works of art produced in this century and still being produced. Indeed, the workshops of all arts are in full swing; we might even be tempted to say: never so active in the past as nowadays. These initial objections to the seriousness of our thesis compel us to formulate the theme in more explicit and deep fashion.

The validity of this theme can only be produced by its results. Our investigation moves from the consideration of a particular work of art, Thomas Mann's *Dr Faustus*.[1] The novel *Dr Faustus* thematises the insoluble difficulties of the artist, his sterility and the death of art, in our world.[2] The same message constitutes the content of the mentor's philosophy. We could, therefore, finally articulate our theme as the question: how are we to think philosophically and justify the philosophical meaning of the *death of art* ? With this question we let art face the abyss of its death. The possibility that art is or might at some stage be no longer alive, shall demand that both art and our reflection on it provide for a fundamental justification of art's validity. By facing the abyss of total negation, we shall inevitably come to a clearer understanding of the nature of art.

In Mann's novel the new Faustus is the musician Adrian Leverkühn: a solitary, severe, coldly rational, deeply proud character. In his youth he studies theology, but not out of interest in divine things. He breaks away from theology and devotes himself entirely to music. In this art, thanks to the devil's favours, Adrian produces works of absolute revolutionary originality and greatness, expressions of an extreme dialectical tension between the opposites: freedom-constriction, chaos-geometry, expression-form, futurism-archaism, divinity-demonicity.[3] The disease, syphilis, is the vehicle of his genius which, without the infection of his nervous-system and without the demonic mediation, would have remained sterile and powerless against the present crisis which paralyses his art.[4] His genius is spent in the sterility of madness.[5] Adrian's life is written by a friend, Serenus Zeitblom, in counterpoint with the chronicles of the barbaric bloody rise of the German people, a rise which ends in a total catastrophe. Serenus remarks and stresses the tragic correspondence of Adrian's life and the signs of the time.

The fact that Thomas Mann thematises in his novel the death of art and the insurmountable difficulties of the modern artist, will be seen more clearly and more cogently, if we considered the diary which accompanied the progressing creation of Mann's *opus magnum. The Genesis of a Novel* [6] indicates and shows how serious and profound were the intentions of the author, when he set to himself the task of proposing the deadly situation in which art and artist find themselves. We should avoid the temptation of containing the novel's content in the sphere of the purely playful, phantastic, imaginative and stylistic game, with no pretension whatsoever to be of any consequence.[7] The *Genesis* will, furthermore, make evident the dilemma embodied in Mann's attempt: to denounce the death of art, by means of a new powerful work of art.[8] Finally, the *Genesis* indicates the underlying presuppositions, the motivations, the elements of historical consciousness which determined the composition of the novel.

The genetical diary begins in 1943: years of war, moment of crisis in European history. "I want to tell the story of *Faustus,* embedded as it is in the pressure and tumult of outward events". These words are Mann's confession and his guiding-line for the project of a novel.[9] Mann's need to reconstruct, by means of his diaries, the constellation of correspondences between his literary work and world happenings, is clear indication of their close relationship. In the diary recurs the refrain of talks and news of war: "Shocking war news", "the dark fate of Germany", "news of the idiotic cruelty of the Nazis".[10] Like a seismographic plate, the *Genesis* records every moment of Mann's insistent, growing consciousness of the *barbarism* overshadowing Europe and threatening the entire world. On the 15 March 1943 Mann decides that the title of his new novel is going to be *Dr Faust*. "The theme was to be some demonic intoxication and its liberating but catastrophic effects, the chief character to be a musician".[11] The basic motif of the novel emerges as *loneliness,* "Solitude, mystic and tragic".[12] "The German solitude in the world. Symbolic values here...", Mann comments.[13]

Meanwhile, the author is working at *Das Gesetz*. In this essay Moses is the main character. "I did not give my hero the features of Michelangelo's Moses but of Michelangelo himself, in order to depict him as an artist toiling over refractory human raw material and suffering dispiriting defeats. The curse at the end, against the present-day wretches to whom power was given to profane his work, the Tables of the Law..."[14] The motifs of Moses-Michelangelo, the laboriously toiling artist, the laboriously toiling wretches, are perfectly in tune with the themes of the novel.

Thomas Mann tells his friends of his intentions. From Neumann he receives enthusiastic encouragement. "What most impressed him was probably the central idea: the flight from the difficulties of the cultural crisis into the pact with the devil, the craving of a proud mind, threatened by sterility, for an unblocking of inhibitions at any cost, and the parallel between the calamitous euphoria ending in a disaster, and the drunkenness of fascist countries".[15] May 23, 1943 *Incipit Faustus*. Thomas Mann, having decided that his hero was to be a musician, planned to study music: "I need the help of a counsellor, of a tutor expert in music, and aware of my intentions". "The helper, adviser, and sympathetic instructor was found, one who through exceptional technical knowledge, and intellectual attainments, was precisely the right person."[16] The mentor is Theodor Wiesengrund Adorno.[17] In July, Mann read very carefully Adorno's manuscript: *Zur Philosophie der moderne Musik,* a study of Schönberg's music. In the manuscript he read "the desperate situation of art", and commented: "this is my man!"[18]

The Genesis, if the novel itself were not eloquent enough, tells us how major events in the history of our century have inspired, nourished and motivated the *poetic* preoccupations of Thomas Mann. *Dr Faustus* can well be regarded as a poetic *summa* of Europe at war, indeed of Twentieth century Europe. Faustus ends his life in madness. Evil and sterility overcome.[19] The *Genesis* has allowed us a deeper understanding of Mann's intentions, and of the historical motivations to write the novel. Such motivations, however, are not to be taken only in their most immediate and particular dimension. In other words, it would not be correct to contain Mann's thematisation of the artist's difficulties and of the death of art, in a horizon of German problems and of the history of the German people: Godless, demoniac, proud, author of barbaric experiences and catastrophically doomed.

In his novel, Mann brings to the highest degree of intensity and clarity the drama of his witnessing *unhappy consciousness:* the consciousness that art and reality, artist and world, are unreconcilable opposites, estranged and enemies to each other; they speak two different languages and constitute contents of experience which are dissonant to each other.[20]

Signs of the *unhappy consciousness* run through the entire production of Thomas Mann. Long before the second-world-war and the completion of *Dr Faustus,* Mann had been aware of the artist's tragic vocation and situation in the world.[21] Think of how the *heroes* in Mann's masterpieces are almost always tragic and solitary artists, condemned to solitude, fighting against difficulties and danger of sterility. Think of

Gustav Aschenbach, the accomplished writer who, having reached the apex of his literary career, longs for a new fecundity, is enchanted by the apparition and presence of a handsome boy, and nurtures his feelings and dreams suddenly become adolescent. Tonio Kröger says of himself that he is deluded and tormented, "somebody who is lost and exiled", "a bourgeois who got lost in art". Art is exile and malediction, a curse for Tonio Kröger. The *Buddenbrooks,* epic end of bourgeoisie, is the "fruit of his (Mann's) resentful solitude", as Mann himself confesses.

It is clear that presuppositions of the *unhappy consciousness* are not lacking in Mann's poetics before the creation of *Dr Faustus*. We might still ask: is this unhappy artistic consciousness uniquely Mann's essential experience, or uniquely a German heritage? Is it only motivated by particular events of recent history? Far from it. Signs of the same unhappy consciousness can be easily found in the creative experience of all great artists of our time, and in the same structure of all great works of our time. They can be found in the literature of all languages, and they appeared long before the years of the second world war. We shall recall to our attention in a very immediate way, some such witnessing signs.

Keats wrote to his friend Woodhouse: "A poet is the most unpoetical of any thing in existence; because he has no identity..." (27th Oct. 1818). Goethe's *Torquato Tasso* is a solitary artist who like a silk worm spins from his innermost the delicious cocoon of poetry until he will be wrapped in it "as in a coffin". Kafka speaks of the artist as of "a bird in a cage", an impossible, absurd bird, a crow (*kavka*) as grey as ashes, which longs to disappear among the stones. Art "challenges the terrifying side of life". In art "the hand protended to touch the world, will be suddenly withdrawn as if it had touched fire". In Kafka's *Diaries* we read: "all is phantasy: family, work, friends, the road; phantasy, far or near, is the woman. But the nearest truth is that you press your head against the wall of a prison-cell without windows and without doors". Garcia Lorca said of himself, as a poet, "I am a sleepless solitude" which longs to find in death "a peaceful solitude". Quasimodo sings the solitude: *Ognuno sta solo sul cuor della terra trafitto da un raggio di sole, ed e subito sera.* In *Thanathos Athanathos* he cries his anguished invocation: "God of silence open the solitude!". The *Glasperlenspiel,* by Hesse, projects the world of all arts, as a citadel which has escaped the total decadence of the world, and is still always constantly threatened by the changes and wars in the outer world. The hero Joseph Knecht, former Master of the Game, goes back to the world in order to offer some indications of truth, of the true sense of history and of the perfect life. But he dies in a gelid alpin lake. Disappears.[22]

The few witnesses we have just been listening to, seem to agree as to the problematic character of art and the artist. They seem to point towards our thematic question: the death of art. We could attune our question to the poetic interrogation of Hölderlin: "What is the good of poets in a barren time?". That we, perhaps even more than Hölderlin, ought to ask such a faithful question, should be clear to all who remember the sad powerful meeting and embrace of the great poets, T S Eliot and Paul Valery, in a very dark day of 1944. "Europe is ended", said Valery. And Eliot responded: "Yes, at least much has ended of what we have until now called Europe". Eliot was thus recreating the meaning of that verse in which he sings of an end which is a beginning.

Europe, much of Europe, is finished. Around us breathes the desert, the *need;* a desert never known to our fathers, or at least never as wide as now. This experience of an end made Kafka exclaim: "The fathers were in the desert, but the desert was not in them, and this is music".[23] The motif of the desert finds it most tragic and violent formulation in Nietzsche's words: "The desert grows...Woe to those who defend the desert!".

The *Unhappy Consciousness* is not an isolated and marginal phenomenon, it is not an experience stemmed from isolated historical events. All modern art gives evidence of the universality of this experience. In particular, *Dr Faustus* thematises the solitude, the desert where life is difficult to grow, and death makes an easy prey of all. The *Genesis* thematises the preoccupation with the "impending sterility". The novel is a development of the motif of the *end.* Serenus writes: "My tale is hastening to its end, like all else today".

What is the meaning of our question about the death of art? Which fundamental vision, pre-vision, has determined Mann's poetics of sterility and solitude? What is the meaning of the warning: "the desert grows"? We cannot exempt ourselves from the task of asking such questions. Because we do not intend to "defend the desert". If there is a *desert,* we need to recognise its threatening nature. It is a matter of consequence: a matter of life or death for art, for the reflection on art, for philosophy of art.

It is time to question *Faustus'* mentor and his philosophy.[24] His philosophy has for us a literary interest, insofar as Adorno contributed in the making of as literary masterpiece[25]; it has an hermeneutical interest, insofar as it allows us a more accurate reading of the novel. But, what is even more interesting, the analysis of Adorno's philosophy will illustrate an essential determination of art, a determination which seems to us to be so easily and so light-heartedly lost sight of. The radical affinity between the philosophical content of Adorno's doctrine and the poetic contents of Thomas Mann's novel, gives evidence of and concretely illustrates that profound, easily forgotten, statement in Hegel's *Aesthetik,* which sounds: "in art we are not simply dealing with a purely pleasant or useful game, but...with a disclosing of truth".[26] Adorno has proposed this statement as frontispiece to his work, *Die Philosophie der neuen Musik*[27], whose first part was read by Mann, when still a manuscript, with great care and attention. Most evident traces of his attentive reading can be easily found through the whole novel, and particularly in the *musical chapters,* Seventh and Twenty Second, and in chapter Twenty Five where the devil propounds, in dialogue with Adrian, his very accurate aesthetics of modern art.[28]

The first part of the *Philosophie* is a philosophical analysis of Schönberg's music and of his disciples, Berg and Webern; the second part dealing with Stravinsky. Schönberg's music is by Adorno masterfully interpreted in its development which begins with an expressionistic poetics, free atonality, and ends in its opposite: cogent constructivity, dodecaphonic law. The music of the *New School of Vienna* is interpreted, through an accurate reading of all its dimensions, as movement and odyssey of subjectivity, human subject and freedom, in the modern world.[29] Schönberg's expressionism overcomes tonal tradition which, from a technical point of view, can only offer worn-out materials; and, from the formal and stylistic point of view, speaks the language of a no longer existing world: a playful, peaceful, satisfied world in which masters and servants, totality and individuality, coexist to the advantage of every form of authority and collectivity.

Expressionism[30] is the chaotic moment of subjectivity aware of being threatened by the forces which determine the movement of contemporary history. These forces, in our days so much overgrown in strength, are: capitalism, industrialism, technology with its computers, politics, bureaucracy, and the modern state tending to become and to be totalitarian. Expressionism is the awakening, with a cry of anguish, to one's own suffering of being a subject threatened with alienations. Opposing itself to the universal process of *reification*[31], the subject finds its freedom. Adorno's analyses of *Erwartung* and *Die glückliche Hand* propose the essential profile of the truth-content to be found in Schönberg's expressionism. Such a truth-content is a *denouncement* articulated in different moments. Here we can only, for a purpose of clarity, schematically summarise these constitutive moments.

1. Total emancipation from tonality and escape from the character of *nature* in music: emancipation disclosing itself as freedom from and over the *materials* of music.

2. Critique of the *appearance,* which proved to be the impetus towards truth; truth being the *real suffering* of man in an alienating world: subversive, chaotic, frantic fragmentation of man's experience into psychotic motions.

3. Abandonment of the stylistic *idiom* (sclerotic, conventional, academic way of composing) to the advantage of a free exercise of *language.*

4. Solitude, which expresses the resistance of the individual subject to being reduced to the false harmony of the objectifying *totality*. Consequent vindication of the rights of particularity: the sounds are redeemed from the totalising tonal domain and supremacy. Dissonance.[32]

Adorno brings to light the dialectical conflict taking place in and constituting structure and content of Schönberg's expressionistic works. Schönberg tries to bring to a final solution the new process for which freedom takes the place of nature; the subjective composition breaks the resistance of mummified musical materials; the artist's isolation disregards the false, artificial, manipulated socialisation; the language overcomes the idiomatic, conventional style; the fragmentation supplants the synthesis; the dissonance supersedes the harmonic-diatonic consonance.

But, having reached the highest degree of liberation from tradition, Schönberg is compelled to determine new laws which take the place of the ancient and superseded ones. To expressionistic *chaos* succeeds dodecaphonic *geometry*. It is the same necessity of freedom regained that compels freedom to posit new laws. No freedom could express itself concretely, without laws.[33] Thus is born the "composition with twelve sounds which are only in relation to each other", dodecaphony. The raw, almost amorphous materials that the expressionistic materials has liberated, find their source of order and cohesion in the dodecaphonic *serial* organisation of sounds. Here the distinction and subordination of servant-sounds and master-sounds is abolished. All sounds, individually, are endowed with the same weight and importance. The Ninth Symphony is taken back![34]

Still, in spite of the new dignity with which each individual sound is endowed, in the dodecaphonic composition every sound is determined by the *series*: "there is no longer *free* notes".[35] Nature, materials, socialisation, style and idiom, synthesis and consonance, all *aufgehoben,* in expressionism, in dodecaphony regain, in a new way, their old and for a moment lost supremacy. In Schönberg's serial compositions it is once again the subjective elements in music that are *relativised:* freedom, inspired and independent composing, the artist's isolation, language, fragmentation and dissonance, are taken over and superseded by the above mentioned *objective* moments and forces of music. Dodecaphony, result of the most progressive and revolutionary freedom, and will-to-freedom, proves itself to be an even more atrocious and severe constriction than the previous laws could ever impose on the materials and on the artist. The highest degree of freedom turns dialectically into its opposite. The extreme points meet. The sounds, so free from and independent of any acoustic-harmonic determination, are enchained by the most severe laws of composition. "Music, fallen prey of the historical dialectics, takes part in this process: and dodecaphony is really its destiny".[36] The subjective project for a final conquest of freedom, fails. The most radical disciple of Schönberg, namely Anton Webern, composes music which approaches silence. Alban Berg is compelled to look back nostalgically to the past, in order to find in it suggestions of the sweet, sad resignation; trying to escape sterility and impossibility.

But, on this point Adorno is most decisive, it is not the artist as such to fail, to fall prey to sterility, to be unable to express the freedom of the subject. It is history that prevents him from succeeding. It is the world in which the artist lives that kills the roots of a free original expression and inspiration to sing. The artist, not less than the materials he works upon, is determined by the same presuppositions that constitute the modern world. What are these presuppositon, these forces of our world, unique and essential of the modern world? We have already mentioned some of them. But what is their meaning? How can they be so threatening of art with sterility, and in some cases even succeed in killing art?

In his *Philosophie der neuen Musik,* and therefore as mentor of Thomas Mann, Adorno was only developing an investigation which began in his youth, in dialogue with Nietzsche, Marx, Hegel, Kant; re-echoing, even though with different intentions, the theses of O. Splengler, J. Huizinga, Husserl and Heidegger, perhaps even Jaspers and Marcel.[37] The investigation had matured musically at the school of Alban Berg, and had finally been clarified and completed in the common work with Max Horkheimer: *Dialektik der Aufklärung,* written in the biennium 1942/44.[38]

The *Philosophie,* by explicit suggestion of the author, must be understood as the *digression* and a development of the *Dialektik.*[39] This work discusses the essence of the *Enlightenment* and of history, from the point of view of a critical examination of our world, and of its genesis. The thesis is gripping. The development of the West, from homeric Greece, is a progressive development of human intelligence, "thought in continuous progress", therefore: progressive conquest of freedom from nature and mastery over nature, escape and liberation from *myths,* from the dark, fearful, natural existence, towards the conquest of *illuminations.*[40] The final stage of such a progress is born with Francis Bacon's project for *una scientia universalis,* which is not concerned with *truth* but with *operation,* functionality, effective procedures and methods for manipulating nature.[41] The motif of *scientia universalis* is re-echoed by Descartes' *Discours de la Methode* where, at the Sixth chapter, he speaks of *des connaissances qui soient fort utiles à la vie;...et ainsi nous rendre comme maîtres et possésseurs de la Nature.* With Bacon and Descartes is born our *brave new world,* our technological world, which is the apex of progress, the apex of Enlightenment. Being the *world* understood not as a *thing* and not even as the complex of things and persons, but being the *world,* the *how* man opens himself, addresses himself to reality, thus constituting reality; the technical world, the horizon or total outlook which this world is, means and is constituted by the basic presupposition that "reality is seen in function of the subject". The true and the real is what the *I*—the *Ego*—produces. This is the essence of what is called *the technical world.*[42]

In this light are to be understood the universal phenomena of industrialisation, the universal process of world-administration. This is the world of the machine, of the computer, of the reifying constriction, of mathematical thinking. It is an alienating world, all enclosed in the sphere of *functioning,* in which the artist feels homeless and in difficulties, and art is always near the abyss of sterility. Because the machine and *functioning* leave no place for freedom and for the spirit. They advocate and enforce the law of *always-the-same,* thus killing the possibility of the *new,* the originality and spontaneity of genius. If this is the case, we should come to the conclusion that art is not a *force* and a *value* in our world. Our world is not an artistic one.[43] With this, Adorno devotes an entire chapter to *cultural industry,* to show how even the most spiritual of our activities are being manipulated, so that they keep only the manifestations of freedom and means of education to freedom[44], *Aufklärung* comes to exhibit its real identity, it proves to be a new *myth* and a new constriction. It proves to be, of its own nature, a dialectical movement. The most advanced stage of progress indicates clear signs of extreme regression. The progress is, at once, a regression. Our world, so nicely arranged and administered, so rich in scientific achievements which help us to live better, is the same world that constantly represses individual subjects, violently negates all human values, barbarically kills and destroys bodies and souls. The wars of our century, there is always one of them!, are only signs, and what eloquent, weighty, bodily, unforgetable signs they are! Our world, so enlightened, so full of intelligence, threatens and negates man and his dignity. In a world like this, art can and must only protest, must only denounce and negate the false light which is in fact darkness.[45] This is the incandescent, magnetic message of *Dialektik der Aufklärung* and of *Philosophie der neuen Musik.* Adorno's later position will be even stronger. Referring to Auschwitz, symbol and citadel of our barbaric world, he pronounces the verdict: "To write poetry after Auschwitz is barbaric. And this corrodes even the knowledge of why it has become impossible to write poetry today. Absolute reification, which presupposed intellectual progress as one of its elements, is now preparing to absorb the mind entirely. Critical intelligence cannot be equal to this challenge as long as it confines itself to self-satisfied contemplation".[46] Even later, in his *Negative Dialektik,* giving an answer to superficial criticisms moved against his much too provocative and scandalous condemnation of art to death, Adorno wrote: "The unceasing suffering has as much right to express itself, as a tortured man has a right to cry; for this reason perhaps it is false to say that after Auschwitz it is impossible to write poetry. But then is not false the less academic question, whether it is still possible, after Auschwitz, to go on living, particularly when one could go on living, who has escaped by chance and, according to rule, should have been liquidated".[47] What is here named is the shame that life carries in itself, after such a degradation of life and loss of human dignity.[48] In those last words of Adorno is also expressed the most consequent position that could be held by a critical mind which is looking for the sense of history in history itself. And the last position cannot be but the most radical pessimism.

Still, in spite of the provocative tone of Adorno's doctrine and its alarming nature and, perhaps, despairing results, instead of dismissing in advance such a philosophy, one should have the courage of going all the way along with the philosopher. The *nondum matura est* of the immortal fox, would be an insufficient and weak criterion in philosophy. In this sense, we take that in Adorno's doctrine is to be found a real and authentic need of our minds, in our modern world. Adorno's philosophy is a search for the truth of our world. His thoughts are in tune with the poetic images of the author of *Dr Faustus*.

We shall now articulate some final, brief reflections. The question of the *death of art* has opened the space for a deeper understanding of our art and of our world. Art is seriously jeopardised and already victim of sterility, because the world is a *desert* in which art could not be but *homeless*. In our world, art is estranged, alienated, outside of its proper element. By confessing its own *homelessness,* art makes sensible, tangible the truth of our world which is homelessness.

Art, modern art, is wounded and tormented, and cannot be healed. Its very nature is *contradiction*. Its truth-content is the falsity of our world. The desert grows...And art, cruel Samaritan, witnesses, denounces and negates this monstrous growth. In a negative, alienating world, art can only be protest and negation. Only and just in this way, the disturbing, no longer beautiful, broken art of our century is *true* art, and the only art that could hope to keep and guard a moment of truth in our dark days. Our art can only trust our negative power: to negate all negations of spirit. Its negativity is the guarantee of its truthfulness.

Art indicates and shows symptoms of death. And still, in the horizon of our technical, dispirited world, in the universal *homelessness,* the need for art is a burning one. There is never so much need for art as when art is near to being suffocated by the ever-growing desert. Negating the negativity of the world, art proves its vocation to be witness of transcendence: "messenger of eternity imprisoned in time", *in confine temporis et aeternitatis,* as Pasternak and St Thomas would say of man himself. Art witnesses the need for spirit.

The question of the death of art has thus moved towards its dialectical opposite. The danger of its death has shown the characters of its true life. Art's life today is the task of making us aware of the desert world, and of resisting it, thus witnessing to the need for transcendence. Art can only be a *voice crying in the desert.*

Pointing at the death of art, Thomas Mann and his mentor, Theodor Wiesengrund Adorno, have brought to light essential determinations of the truth of modern art, which is also the truth of modern man in the modern world.

Structuralism, Avant-Garde, Semiotics

*The only faith that the aesthetics and
metaphysics of the Chaosmos leaves us is
the faith in contradiction.* (Umberto Eco)

*The century of the aeroplane is entitled to
its own music.* (Debussy)

The problematic nature and vocation of art in an unjust, un-pacified,
conflictual and *administered* world, as outlined in Adorno's writings on
music, in particular, is a theme explored, from an entirely different
perspective, by the distinguished structuralist ethnologist, Claude Lévi-
Strauss. While Adorno, as a dialectical thinker, upholds the critical intentions of avant-garde poetics, in its extreme tendencies; Lévi-Strauss,
as a structural anthropologist, rejects the poetics of avant-garde, for it
questions the very intentions of the structuralist project and of the
structuralist understanding of culture. We could say that the poetics of
avant-garde and the structural methodology, represented respectively by
Adorno and Lévi-Strauss, as extreme advocates of the two tendencies,
instance and imply two radically opposed philosophical projects. While
avant-garde poetics, as philosophical disposition, aims at shaping reality,
at changing history, by pursuing the progressive production of ever new
messages; structural thought tries to discover, regressively and nostalgically, some kind of original and mythical code that would allow us to
interpret history and to understand culture as a closed system of communication.

In the light of our exploration into Adorno's philosophy of avant-
garde music, this chapter will present the analysis of Lévi-Strauss' radical criticism of avant-garde. The aim of this analysis is to show that the
claims of both critical theory and structural methodology, can be better
understood from a higher-viewpoint: a more neutral, more universal
and more sophisticated methodology. I mean, of course, semiotic discourse.

In the Overture to *The Raw and the Cooked*[1] Lévi-Strauss mounts a ferocious attack against Twentieth century art, particularly non-figurative, abstract and informal painting, on the one hand, and against serial music and *musique concrète,* on the other hand. He labels avant-garde art and its expressions by the general name of *serialist thought* which he contrasts to *structural thought.* And we must remark that the renowned anthropologist conceives structuralism and serialism not simply as stylistic and methodological options, but as fundamental and ultimate world-views, epistemic and metaphysical models.

By criticising avant-garde or serialist poetic solutions, from the viewpoint of structuralism, Lévi-Strauss aims at proving that: 1) avant-garde art is bad art and even not art at all; 2) that the epistemic and metaphysical model which avant-garde presupposes and expresses is untenable; finally, 3) that structuralism is the model best suited to explain myth, language, art, music, the totality of culture and the totality of reality.

In order to better appraise the claims and criticisms of Lévi-Strauss, I shall outline a brief survey of structuralism as a methodology. Originally practiced in linguistics by Ferdinand de Saussure, structuralism became more fashionable in philosophy and anthropology, in the Fifties and Sixties, as a critical and polemical response to the claims of existentialism which emphasised individualism, an extreme and paradoxical concept of freedom, consciousness, subjectivity, spontaneity and creativity. In brief, according to structuralism: 1) consciousness is only the deformed and mistaken reflex of subconscious mechanisms; 2) subjectivity is only the product of the impersonal linguistic order through which communication is made possible; 3) the individual, rather than an active, free and autonomous agent, is only a meeting-point (a *point de capiton,* to quote Lacan) and a casual vehicle of matrixes, grids, structures that fundamentally determine him. This last point suggests that, according to structuralism, nothing is understandable and knowable, if taken in isolation, precisely because the individual value and meaning can only be grasped if seen "in opposition", as Saussure would say, to another value or meaning, and hence fundamentally dependent and determined by the structure of relations within which it is situated. In other words, knowledge and understanding consist in discovering or in positing an underlying common structure or system of relations among apparently unrelated facts or events. In the light of this, structuralism argues that the human world and the spiritual sciences should be investi-

79

gated in the same manner in which we study the natural world and the natural sciences. Structuralist methodology proceeds by positing hypothetical models for the explanation of multiple spheres of reality or experience apparently unrelated, but deep down and in the end logically reducible to co-relating orders. Hence, structuralism does not and should not presume or promise to know what the structured object is really, in reality or ontologically. Structuralism claims only to hypothesise, or in some cases actually discover by deduction, invariable forms or models applicable to different sets of experience.

If we were to attempt a definition, we would say that the *structure* is a model as a system of differences, capable of transformations and transpositions which allow its applicability to diverse orders of phenomena. To quote P. Bridgam: "the model is a useful and inevitable tool for thought, insofar as it allows us to think of unfamiliar realities in terms of familiar realities and experiences".[2] In consequence, the structure represents an impoverishment of reality. It is a simplification resulting from the decision to apply a particular and hypothetical point of view, in an attempt to map reality. The structure is an artificial, abstract, arbitrary and hypothetical way of grasping different objects in a homologous fashion. If we think of a structure as a blueprint and a map, we can also clearly appreciate the meaning of the by now proverbial warning that "the map is not the territory". From a structure applicable to a chosen set of homogeneous phenomena, the structuralist would proceed to hypothesise a deeper structure applicable to that set and to yet another set of phenomena apparently unrelated to the first. After this operation we can ask whether we should hypothesise a further deeper structure of the deep structure, such that it may allow extended applicability to an increasingly wider order of phenomena.

Structural ethnologists and anthropologists, following the precepts of structural linguistics, proceed in this very fashion. Having defined the structure of a particular *language*, they seek a deeper structure or code capable of explaining the first structure and that of another language. Consequently, they seek a further deeper code which may allow, for instance, the comparison between the internal relations of a language and the relations obtaining in the language or system of kinship, the disposition of huts in a given village, the rules of cooking, eating, washing, dressing, myth-telling, music-making, and any other kind of human experience or cultural event. From simplification to symplification, the structuralist finally dreams to find the *Structure* of all structures, the *Code* of all codes: the *Primordial Structure*. This would allow the discovery of the elementary operations and interactions in the context of every possible form of human behaviour: from the most natural, physical and biological, to the most culturally mediated and sophisticated. This *Primordial Structure* and *Primordial Code* ought to be, according to Lévi-Strauss, identified with the very mechanisms of the human mind. "According to Lévi-Strauss, all structures should be reducible to the mind's structure, for they are nothing else but *temporal modalities of the universal laws in which consists the unconscious activity of the mind*".[3]

After this step, however, Structuralism ceases to be a method only, and metamorphoses into a realist philosophy and a kind of ontology. The structure, from being a purely logical and hypothetical construct, turns into the real and ontological order of being. The primordial structure, as explanatory principle of all reality, turns out to be a hypostatic, fixed principle which determines our evaluation of cultural, artistic and historical processes. The structure comes to be identified with *Objective Thought* which thinks itself through us, through myths, through language.

An examination of Lévi-Strauss's *Overture*, especially of the arguments concerning the nature of music and the critique of avant-garde, will illustrate, more concretely, the method and the limitations of structuralism. By means of dialectical argument, by rejecting as untenable the presuppositions adopted by Lévi-Strauss and therefore also the conclusions of his arguments, we will be in a better position to highlight the characteristic features of avant-garde poetics.

The first argument runs as follows: myth and music are isomorphous systems, they have similar structures, because they are *languages*, in general, or systems of communication. Furthermore, myth and music are both isomorphous of natural language, specifically, or articulate speech. Interestingly, Lévi-Strauss speaks of "the existence of an isomorphism between the mythic system, which is of a linguistic order, and the system of music which, as we know, constitutes a language, since we understand it".

In his passionate search for isomorphisms or underlying structures, Lévi-Strauss is anxious to stress the formal similarity of music, myth and articulate speech. The common denominator is *language*, the common structure is the structure of *language* as a system of communication. Music, like myth and like articulate speech or natural language in the strict sense, is a *language* "since we understand it". Taken in its generic and unqualified form, the argument is acceptable also because, in the end, it is actually tautological or analytic, as Kant would put it. If *language*, in general, is a system of communication, every kind of communication implies that it is a kind of *language*. Music is a kind of communication, "since we understand it", hence music is a kind of language. The same goes for myth and for *natural language* or articulate speech, hence music has something in common, is isomorphic with both myth and articulate speech. We would say, in semiotic terms, that myth, music, natural languages are instances or *tokens* of the general type language as universal and abstract system of communication. However, as we shall see in greater detail, Lévi-Strauss forces the argument and, by means of an illicit and unwarranted transposition or logical transition, identifies the structure of musical discourse with the structure of natural language or articulate speech. We must also note that, in his pursuit for similarities and isomorphisms, Lévi-Strauss does not hesitate to naively assert, without further explanation, that: "music arouses similar ideas in different brains". I am quite sure that this is not the case. Lévi-Strauss, for his part, makes no attempt at convincing us by proving or, at least, by illustrating his claim.

What is of particular significance for us is that the insistence upon the isomorphism to be found (or postulated?) in music, myth, natural language, and the unwarranted, surreptitious identification of music and articulate speech, aim at a polemical criticism of avant-garde poetics. According to Lévi-Strauss, myth, music, natural language "involve reference to general structures that serialist doctrine rejects..." More explicitly:

> Music and mythology appeal to mental structures that the different listeners have in common. The point of view I have adopted involves therefore reference to general structures that serialist doctrine rejects and whose existence it even denies. On the other hand, these structures can only be termed general if one grants them an objective foundation...whereas serial music sets itself up as a conscious product of the mind and an assertion of its liberty.

As I have already mentioned, when Lévi-Strauss speaks of serialist thought he polemises not only against new music, but against all forms of avant-garde. In particular, he mentions abstract, non-representational and informal painting, and argues that painting should be the imitation of reality and of real objects easily recognisable in the painting. Indeed, he speaks of a "congenital subjection of the plastic arts to objects", and of their "state of subjection to the world of sense experience and its organisation in the form of objects". In other words, the primordial law of the visual arts is that the works should represent reality, according to our author.

> The first question that springs to the mind of someone looking at a picture is: what does it represent? But if the problem is formulated in this way at the present time, we are faced with the anomaly of non-figurative painting.

Non-figurative painting, by employing colours, lines, forms, without reference to objects "would inevitably take on a decorative character".

> Without ever fully existing in its own right, it would become anemic, unless it attached itself to objects as adornment, while drawing its substance from them. It is, then, as if painting had no other choice but to signify beings and things...

If Lévi-Strauss were right, most of this century's visual and plastic art would have to be considered decoration. Artists like Braque, Mondrian, Kandinsky and Klee, Picasso, Gris, Rothko, Miro, Burri...to mention but the most obvious, would equally deserve to be called decorators rather than artists...

Let us clarify the reason why Lévi-Strauss could reach such unreasonable conclusions. His argument is grounded on a linguistic presupposition, namely: the idea of the double level of articulation. He borrows the idea from Saussure's theory of linguistics. Language *as articulate speech* is made up of words or morphemes that carry meaning; and the words are made up of letters of the alphabet, or phonemes, that carry no meaning. "Morphemes, which are significant elements, break down into phonemes, which are articulatory elements without significance". This is how *natural language* is structured. This is what must also take place, isomorphically and necessarily, in the language of painting and the language of music, according to Lévi-Strauss. According to him, furthermore, painting and music differ from articulate speech in some accidental respects, but, like natural language which best exemplifies the *Primordial Structure of Thought,* they ought to be constituted by the structural double level of articulation. In the case of painting, then, the morphemic, significant or meaningful, level would consist in the referential, representational character of the totality and of the parts of the individual painting. The painting would carry meaning because of its "subjection to the world of sense experience and its organisation in the form of objects". The secondary level of articulation, the phonemic level, would be constituted by the colours and lines which are natural properties of objects but have no meaning in themselves. Obviously, abstract and informal painting abandons any referential, descriptive and representational intention. Hence, it refuses to portray or denote objects.

> It can thus be understood why abstract painting and more generally all schools of painters claiming to be non-figurative lose the power to signify: they abandon the primary level of articulation and assert their intention of surviving on the second alone.

Abstract, informal, non-representational painting, in other words, ceases to be a *language*, as a means of communication, because it violate and defies the structure of *natural language*: the double level of articulation. Insofar as music is concerned, the same claims and the same identification between it and natural language, are made

> We can say that music operates according to two grids. One is physiological—that is natural: its existence arises from the fact that music exploits organic rhythms and thus gives relevance to phenomena of discontinuity that would otherwise remain latent and submerged, as it were, in time. The other grid is cultural: it consists of a scale of musical sounds, of which the number and the intervals vary from one culture to another. The system of intervals provides music with an initial level of articulation, which is a function not of the relative heights of the notes, but of the hierarchical relations among them on the scale; the division into fundamental, tonic, dominant, and leading notes expresses relations that the polytonal and atonal systems complicate but do not destroy. The composer's mission is to modify the discontinuity without challenging its principle.[4]

We note that, according to Lévi-Strauss, the system of intervals constitutes one of the two levels of articulation. More interestingly, we must remark that the principle of the hierarchical relations among the notes on the scale is here identified exclusively with the harmonic code of tonal music. And that principle should not be challenged! But we hasten to qualify that the mentioned division into fundamental, tonic, dominant, for instance, is tenable and pertinent within the context of harmonic theories *à la Rameau*. The same division, however, does not obtain and is neither relevant nor pertinent in other musical systems and traditions belonging to cultures other than modern European culture. The division and pertinent differentiation between fundamental, tonic,

84

dominant, does not obtain in modal music (be it Medieval plain chant or Greek and Jewish musical syntax), in oriental, middle and far, music in general, in percussion African music.

Lévi-Strauss is correct in stating that polytonal systems complicate but do not destroy the relations among intervals conceived in the context of harmonic fields. But this is quite obvious to anybody who knows the meaning of the word poly-tonality! Insofar as atonal, better free-tonal, music is concerned, I understand that it does not destroy hierarchical relations sustained by the theory of harmony, but it certainly suspends and frustrates the laws of harmonic gravitation and attraction. I could add that even serial music, not mentioned in this context, does not actually destroy the harmonic-tonal structure and codification of sounds. It simply expands, questions and hence supersedes that structure and that code, by *doing something else*: inventing and positing a new code, a new structure, by uttering new messages.

Lévi-Strauss is, however, insensitive to a more supple, tolerant, historically literate and pluralistic conception of art in general and of music in particular. As we have already seen, for him music and painting are *languages*. Therefore, he argues as a structuralist, they must be articulated according to a structure similar to that of natural language or articulate speech. This is made up of two levels of articulation. Consequently music and painting must also be structured according to two levels of articulation. If music and painting fail to do so, they fail to be meaningful and they fail to be languages...! Hence they also fail, *a fortiori*, to deserve the name of art.

Lévi-Strauss does not tire to repeat, and hence to increase the embarrassment of his critical stance, that: "It is precisely in the hierarchical structure of the scale that the first level of articulation of music is to be found". *Musique concrète,* for instance, wipes out the first level of articulation, by substituting hierarchically organised sounds with noises. To be precise, Lévi-Strauss adds that if *musique concrète* utilised noises as noises, without filtering and manipulating them electronically, then it would still have "at its disposal a first level of articulation (for, we hasten to add, noises can be referential and denotative, in the manner of Peirce's *indexes)* which would allow it to set up a system of signs through the bringing into operation of a second articulation. But this system would allow almost nothing to be said". Let us analyse the manner in which Lévi-Strauss illustrates (and attempts to prove?) the validity of his last statement:

> To be convinced of this, one has only to imagine what kind of stories could be told by means of noises, with reasonable assurance that such stories would be both intelligible and moving.

I find this argument particularly naive, sophistical and quite absurd. I mean: since when is music supposed to "tell stories, both intelligible and moving"? Not so naively, Lévi-Strauss is careful enough to avoid the simple identification of *musique concrète* and serial music. He acknowledges that twelve-tone or serial music has a subtle and complex syntax, a complex set of compositional rules, a complex code at its disposal; and that, therefore, it remains within the bounds of music proper. But soon he adds a contradictory argument marked, to my mind, by sheer ignorance.

> The serial approach, by taking to its logical conclusion that whittling down of the individual particularities of tones...seems to tolerate only a very slight degree of organisation of the tones.

The first part of this statement is an ill-informed misrepresentation. For, as I understand, by overcoming and questioning the traditional code of harmonic relations, serial music precisely aims to and succeeds in foregrounding and liberating the individuality of each musical element and the particularity of each individual tone. Indeed, serial music treats individual sound/tones as acoustic microcosms to be exploited as rigourously polyphonic and contrapunctal parts, and to be explored in their manifold aspects and in their indefinite expressive possibilities.[5] The second part of the statement is clearly false. The final argument against serial music and the thought which it embodies and expresses are grounded, again, on the *linguistic* nature of music and therefore its obligation, according to our distinguished ethnologist, to adopt and preserve the two levels of articulation characteristic of articulate speech or *natural language*. With misdirected obstinacy, Lévi-Strauss insists in unjustifiably identifying *language* with *natural languages* and with any language, as if it were an obvious fact. "The fact is that in the case of *any language* the first level of articulation is immovable". And again, abstract painting, *musique concrete* and serial music are, all alike, "trying to construct a system of signs on a single level of articulation".

I shall try, now, to sum up the argument put forward by Lévi-Strauss. *The Primordial Structure,* the model of all models, and the code of all codes, is identified with the *Universal Mechanisms* of the human *Mind* as *Objectified Thought.*[6] Objectified thought, the totality of culture, is in turn identified with the dual articulation of Language as in articulate speech or natural language. Every other language, which makes up the totality of culture, must reproduce the primordial code of language: its double articulation! This is Lévi-Strauss's conviction. Alas!, he is wrong. The principle of the double articulation, which works well when applied to the study of natural language, should not be applied and cannot be applied, like a dogma, to other kinds of languages or systems of communication. What would be, for instance, the first or second level of articulation of our body language or proxemics? What could one say about the language of clothing or of scents/perfumes? How could one apply the criterion of the dual level of articulation, to understand the language of card games where, among other aspects, the values change according to different games?[7] The fact is, and this is a real fact!, that language as articulate speech is only one particular instance, token and species of *Language as Communication System* or semiotic system. Other languages, such as indeed music and painting or artistic languages in general, employ different kinds and numbers of articulation. Furthermore, art languages or languages used for the purpose of aesthetic effect, by definition are constituted as indefinite and continuous questioning of previous *articulations*, structures or codes. For instance, in contemporary music, the practice of the so-called *Klangfarbenmelodie* gives evidence of the fact that the colour, a relatively variable and redundant element in traditional music, acquires the value of a highly *pertinent* element, more deeply exploited in all its virtual possibilities. We could also think of the practice of the *Sprechgesang,* the use of ready-made sounds, electronically construed sounds, pre-existent natural noises, prepared sound. Or think of the refined exploitation and manipulation of intensity, attack, density-volume, micro-sounds in an electronic continuum of transition from tone to tone, etc. All these are pertinent traits and elements in contemporary music, while they would be deemed noise, and, in fact, they are not to be found, in the traditional tonal and harmonic systems.

Finally, it seems clear that Lévi-Strauss criticises and fails to understand avant-garde art, in the instances of serial music, *musique concrète,* abstract and non-representational painting, because he identifies the structure of music as a language with one particular, historically situated, code or structure: namely the system of gravitations and attractions of sounds organised according to the principle of harmony (naively and partially understood, anyway). By the same token, he identifies the structure of painting as a language with the particular, historically situated, model and code of representational painting.

Not unlike Hindemith, Ansermet, and the host of traditionalist critics of serial and avant-garde music, Lévi-Strauss believes in perennial and immutable musical codes, natural sounds and natural laws.[8] Unlike structuralism, serialist thought or avant-garde is acutely aware of the relativity and historicity of culture and therefore of art and its languages. The explicit and intentional rejection of the past, as in Impressionism and later in Dada, Surrealism, Futurism, Cubism, Expressionism, Serial music, expresses the artist's dissatisfaction with a language that has exhausted its possibilities. To quote Debussy: "The century of the aeroplane is entitled to its music". The new realities, the new sensibility, the new values, the new knowledge, the new science of the new era cannot be adequately expressed with the old voices.

If, with avant-garde, we witness the break-down of all the classical values in art, we must note that a similar revolution, equally deep, has taken place in the sciences where the traditional concepts of space, matter, gravitation, have been subjected to radical revision and have, by and large, been substituted by new categories such as indeterminacy, relativity, probability, enthropy...With the negation and the obsolescence of past concepts and categories, emerges the need to produce an image of the new era. It is an old principle that art is child of its time. To put it otherwise, quoting Umberto Eco's *The Open Work*, the work of art is an *epistemic metaphor* of its world. In a world, like ours since the turn of the century, in which the discontinuity of phenomena (and their contemporaneous manifold transmission) has undermined the possibility of a unitary, homogeneous, closed and definitive image or map, the work of art will abandon any claim to order, completeness, and beauty, but will rather attempt to suggest a way of seeing what we live. The work of art, in avant-garde, does not describe or recount or celebrate an image of the world. In its form and in its poetic structure, the avant-garde work of art wants to reproduce the image of its world.

Historicism and vitalism, psychoanalysis and the *stream of consciousness,* the theory of relativity and the new sub-atomic physics, the recent technological revolution, the global village, the ubiquity and contemporaneity of mass communication..., all these experiences cannot be adequately recounted by the closed *work* of the past. I find very enlightening the well known anecdote reported by Anton Webern in his *Towards New Music.* In a letter to his poet friend, Hildegard Jone, Webern writes, with obvious excitement: "I have found a series (I mean 12 sounds) that contains a large number of internal correlations (of the 12 sounds among themselves). It is a series somewhat similar to the ancient acrostic:

$$S \quad A \quad T \quad O \quad R$$
$$A \quad R \quad E \quad P \quad O$$
$$T \quad E \quad N \quad E \quad T$$
$$O \quad P \quad E \quad R \quad A$$
$$R \quad O \quad T \quad A \quad S$$

which should be read first horizontally, then vertically, and so on..."

The image of the complexity of the world can be adequately rendered only by a manifold, polyvalent, dynamic and open work of art. With particular reference to music, we must note that a classical composition, whether it be a Bach *Cantata*, Mozart's *Concerti,* Verdi's *Othello*, or Stravinsky's *Rite of Spring*, is made up of sound units which the composer arranged in a closed, inclusive, well defined and structured manner before presenting it to the listener. The interpreters and the listeners are closely guided by the intentions of the composer. Avant-garde compositions, on the contrary, by and large reject the ideal of a definitive, concluded, closed message and rather highlight and multiply the formal possibilities of the distribution and arrangement of their elements. They appeal to the initiative of the performer and of the listener, and hence they present themselves not as finite and closed messages but as ambiguous and open works.[9]

The listener and the performer are invited to subjective acts of conscious freedom. In their formal instability and semantic ambiguity, the avant-garde works of art embody a questioning revision and rejection of tradition, a going-beyond tradition. At once, the avant-garde work of art is constituted as a presentation of its own poetics: the work is about how it came to be formed, it contains the inner logic of its making and the critical revision of that same poetic logic.

The essence of the avant-garde consists in the explicit questioning of the traditional, rational, closed order. Avant-garde is a challenge to the idea and ideal of order: a destruction of previous forms of order, with the resulting invention of a new paradoxical order: the order of probability and discontinuity.[10]

To conclude, I would like to sum up what I have suggested sofar and explain it in semiological terms. Every process of communication, that is of social and cultural exchange of information, can be understood according to the model of a chain of interacting units and elements. In a simplified manner, that chain could be articulated in the following terms:[11]

Source-Sender-Message-Channel-Message-Receiver-Addressee
!---- Code -----!

With reference to this model, the relation between *Code* and *Message* is of particular interest to us. [Saussure would speak of *Langue* and *Parole*. Chomsky's distinction between *Competence* and *Performance* can be understood in the same sense. Finally, *Code* and *Message* could be translated in the terms of Structure and individual Cultural Event]. To give a brief example, the message: *Nel mezzo del cammin di nostra vita,* can be decoded, and hence understood, first and foremost, if not even solely, by reference to the code of the Italian language. Indeed, Dante himself could only write this verse, utter this message, in force of his shared knowledge of the code, grammar and syntax, of his language. If it is true, therefore, that individual messages can be formed and uttered on the basis of a pre-existing code, it is equally true that every message is an instance, an occurrence, a realisation, an actualisation of the code. We could say, in other words, that if there are no messages that are intelligible, that is, communicative and carriers of meaning, without reference to an underlying code; equally so, there are no codes without concrete production of messages. More to the point, messages must not be understood as only re-enactments or instances and determined applications of the generative code.[12] The universe of aesthetic messages, in particular, offers an exemplary instance of the dialectical and dramatic interaction between codes and messages. As we have seen in

90

previous pages, the aesthetic message, while contextualised with reference to familiar codes, presents itself as a questioning of old rules and conventions, and hence as productive of new codes. The aesthetic message, in other words, instances the energy of creativity and the process of revision of any code and of any structure.

From the previous analyses, we may finally outline the distinguishing traits of structural methodology, on the one hand, and of avant-garde poetics, on the other hand.[13] Structuralism, especially as practised by Lévi-Strauss, conceives the relationship between code and message, as one of total dependence of the message from the code. Communication, intelligibility and meaning, occur only insofar as 1) the message corresponds to and is decoded on the basis of a pre-established, inviolable code or structure common to both the speaker and the receiver; 2) every communication implies the adoption of a code based on the double level of articulation (selection and combination; morphemes and phonemes); where the phonemes are less numerous than morphemes, are foreseen by the code's selectivity and are endowed with oppositional values due to their position in the system; 3) every code rests on more fundamental codes, so that every practice of communication can be reduced to a fundamental, unique, primordial Code. This would constitute the real Structure and Code of every possible communication. Messages exist as totally in function of and in dependance from the code.

Serialist thought, and the poetics of avant-garde, on the contrary holds that every message questions and challenges the code. Every message/parole constitutes a discussion of the code/langue that generates it. Finally, and in the extreme, every message posits its own code; each individual work presents itself as the linguistic foundation of itself, as the discussion of its own poetics, as the very key to its own reading, as an act of liberation from previous codes and conventions; 2) messages are not reducible to the code of double articulation, but, especially so in the case of aesthetic messages, are endowed with the character of polysemy, connotation, etc. In particular, the *row* or series, as a constellation, is a field of possibilities, that generates multiple choises and multiple readings: its Openness! It is then possible, for instance, to conceive large and complex and mixed structural or syntagmatic chains [Stockhausen's *Gruppe*, Cage's *Roaratorio*, etc...], the materic heap of action painting, the techniques, since Dada, of assemblage, the manifold and open informal, the transposition of materic elements from a context to another less probable and less familiar context; finally 3) even though it may be the case that every communication rests upon a Primordial Code which allows cultural and social interaction, what really matters, for avant-garde and serial thought, is to single out particular, historically given codes/conventions and to question/challenge them, in order to produce, from their revision, new ways of communicating. Serialist thought and avant-garde art privilege the role of the message and the role of the work as carriers of novelty and expressions of individual freedom. Avant-garde carries the logic of aesthetic creation to its extreme: it must challenge codes and defamiliarise the apparent order of the world, hence estrange the receiver, to the point of extreme experimentation and alienation. Perhaps to the point of silence.

Dante's *Paradiso* and the Aesthetics of Light

O luce eterna che sola in te sidi....

Walter Benjamin suggested, with reference to the reading of poetry in general, that poets and poetry should not be commented upon, but rather be quoted[1] Although the re-enactment through memory and quotation should finally be *the use of poetry,* it would seem, nonetheless, that a preliminary process of interpretation justifies its utility and even necessity. We interpret and comment so that, in the end, we may be able to quote, to quote well, to judiciously know why and what we quote. The preliminary process of interpretation and critical comment is even more necessary when the universal quality of a poetic diction is inseparable from a particular cultural condition quite alien to and far removed from the reader

In one of his precious compositions, J.L. Borges wrote: "Perhaps universal history is the history of some metaphors". And then, at the end of the essay: "Perhaps history is the history of the diverse intonations of some metaphors".[2]

Dante's *Commedia* is doubtless one of the most resounding, universal, complex metaphors of reality, a sublime picture and model of the world, a vast system of metaphors. We could say, with Francesco De Sanctis: *Che cosa e la Commedia? E' il mondo universale del Medioevo realizzato nell 'arte* (What is the *Commedia?* It is the total Medieval world realised in art). The *Commedia,* and perhaps *Paradiso* in particular, synthesises, distils and at once interprets the spirit of the Middle Ages: the taste, the style, the wisdom, the artistic sensibility, the philosophical and theological disposition, the very soul of an era in its full maturity and already approaching its decline.

With good reasons hosts of critics have insisted upon the structural and formal analogies obtaining between the *Commedia* on the one hand and, on the other, the model of philosophical and theological documents, the *summae,* the dynamism of Gothic arches and the compact solidity

93

and simplicity of Romanesque structures, the aesthetic experience of light imprisoned in and reflected by Byzantine mosaics or streaming through the spaces of quasi-immaterial walls and naves, even when filtered by the colours of stained glass. Though quite correct and worth mentioning, these are only superficial, obvious and predictable similarities.

Following the paths of the poet's discourse, the concentric rose of ideas, concepts and metaphors in which we capture the echo of the whole Western tradition (from Plato and Aristotle, through Plotinus, Virgil, Cicero, Augustine and the Fathers, the Arabs, up to Thomas Aquinas), we experience an unavoidable sense of nostalgia, the need to grasp and translate the essential simplicity, the unified economy, the innocent intelligence that unfolds organically and grows into the complete poem. *Paradiso* constitutes the distillation of Medieval theo-philo-sophy, the epistemological metaphor and the conceptual image of an epoch. In this *cantica,* the conceptual and theological discourse (articulated as a chain of ordered analogies) and the metaphorical poetic intuition live symbiotically. Thought-content and poetic diction rest upon the same ground of analogy, the quintessentially Medieval model of experience. This symbiosis and common ground explains why and how Dante could so consistently *poetise,* why the poet could so unerringly find aesthetic solutions, while insistently referring to a precisely defined and culturally identifiable image of an order of the world and to a vast complex of facts, meanings and experiences. The *Commedia* could never be read adequately, solely through the lenses of a formalist approach. Even the critics who find, particularly in *Paradiso,* an excess of ethical, didactic, analogical, symbolic, theoretical preoccupations (which, in their opinion, obscure and stifle the lyrical energy and transparency), finally seem to forget that Dante is a Medieval and that the improbable hypothesis of pure formalism and of *art for art's sake,* which Dante would, of course, consider fatuous, cannot be easily sustained, not even on a purely hypothetical and conceptual level.

Against the critical suggestion that Dante, particularly in his *Paradiso, reasons* too much and hence weakens the power of lyrical vision and diction, by means of excessively rational discourse, I would like to make a preliminary point that might do away with unnecessary preoccupations and help avoid gratuitous pre-judgements. The theo-philo-sophical discourse is, to my mind, systematically and ostensibly self-effaced and self-negated. Dante writes the poem of *cose che ridire/ né sa né puó chi di la su discende* (Things which to relate again,/ Surpasseth power of him who comes from thence). Human theoretical discourse, adequately clad in poetic form, is articulated in order to suggest the silence of intuitive vision. Dante writes poetry, in order to be silent. He reasons, with the cogent rigour typical of his Age, in order to contemplate. The theoretical, intellectual clarity of his disquisitions stands as the adequate counterpoint to, and is at once nourished by the demands of unthinkable and unspeakable mystical experience. This is also nearest and analogically closest to aesthetic contemplation and poetic intuition.

I do not think it is possible to overstress the importance and the poetic power of this aesthetic solution: the unending energy of *praeteritio*. Dante's poetic intention to say what cannot be said, and, paradoxically, his ability to say it, astutely constitutes a fundamental ambiguity that permeates and determines, as matrix, the general movement and the very make-up of the entire *Commedia*, and of the *Paradiso* in particular.

For the Medievals the world is a vast allegory, an analogical system of symbols, to be decoded while being *contemplated*.[3] Dante's *Commedia* is, at once, a poetic *summa* and a theo-philo-sophical poem. It is, perhaps, the most Medieval of all medieval documents. But, although deeply rooted in the theo-philo-sophy of its time, Dante's poem offers a richer vision of reality, truer, we could say, than the image encoded in philosophical and theological documents. For the *Commedia*, which unfolds as a journey of the soul and the odyssey of mankind, articulates itself as the image of existential progress and inner motion, the processual activity of being, the pilgrimage *per lo gran mar dell 'essere* (Through the vast sea of being). I am suggesting that the *Commedia* is sustained and animated by an energetic dynamism not to be found, or not to the same degree at any rate, in the formally rather rigid, because substantialist and essentialist, Medieval theo-philo-sophy.

The journey through *Inferno* is tiresome and laborious, it unfolds through utter darkness only broken by fires. Noise is its background. *Inferno* is inhabited by apparitions rendered in volume, mass and plastic forms. And, as Titus Burckhardt has significantly remarked, the damned are those who have lost *il ben dell 'intelletto* (the power of intellect): the intuition of principles, the immediate vision of the goal and the intuitive, natural nostalgia for God. The damned can, however, *rea-*

son very cogently, they can articulate logically clear, impeccable discourses, though removed from and deprived of the knowledge of principles and of God as supreme Principle. We could note here that also the Blessed (*i beati*), in *Paradiso,* engage in the inevitable exercise of reasoning. However, they do so only in order to explain, to suggest, to hint at the nature of *il ben dell'intelletto* : their beatific vision, their *seeing face to face:* beholding the object of their desire.

Purgatorio, the mountain at dawn, is the realm of self-contained meditation, gentle dialogue, sensitive suggestion of the innermost order and serene self-acceptance of the atoning soul. The movement and the tempo are subtle and regular, like breathing and a peaceful heartbeat. The light is soft, translucid, diaphanous. The atmosphere is perfectly rendered by the precious verses:

> Dolce color d'oriental zaffiro,
> che s'accoglieva nel sereno aspetto
> del mezzo puro infino al primo giro,
> agli occhi miei ricomincio diletto, (*Purg.* I: 13-16).
> (Sweet hue of eastern saphire that was spread o'er the serene aspect of the pure air, high up as the first circle, to mine eyes unwonted joy renew'd).

Purgatorio is a pensive universe of nostalgic twilight, sustained by monodic, humble chant.

In *Paradiso* we enter the realm of jubilant, radiant, exuberant light. And just as Dante cannot see, at first, for the light is too pure and too bright, so we too, as readers, undergo the same experience of frustrated sight, when confronted with the luminous poetry of *Paradiso.* The sharpness of its splendour veils the depth of its beauty. *Paradiso* is inhabited by an overjoyed, powerfully choral community. Its music is symphonic; its space, a timeless transparency; its tempo, an unbroken continuity between soul and soul, Heaven and Heaven (*cielo e cielo*), star and star. The body is glory, light and spirit. The key word, the theme, in its endless variations, is *light*

I would now, first of all, suggest a schematic and possible division of the canto, which may help us to highlight some essential features and foreground some structural elements of the entire *Paradiso.*

1. The opening triplet announces the theme of the canto: *La Gloria di colui che tutto move* (His glory, by whose might all things are moved). The whole canto will unfold as a progressive series of symphonic variations on the theme; an elated celebration of divine light and splendour

and the manifold degrees of God's luminously active presence in the universe.

2. Vv. 4-12: the poet announces the content of his paradisiac experience, though inadequately retained through memory. The mystical vision and its imperfect recollection are announced as the matter of poetic treatment.

3. Vv. 13-36 constitute a lengthy and somewhat preciously wrought invocation and prayer, ostensibly redolent of classical reference, that Apollo/Christ may grant the needed inspiration.

4. Vv. 37-48: by means of a complex and even hermetic astral symbolism, Dante gives us the temporal coordinates of his journey. The ascension through the heavenly spheres begins under most favourable stars. Indeed their position is optimally congenial to influence the human mind. This section is a first major variation on the theme of light. Then Beatrice is introduced, absorbed in contemplation, gazing into the sun: *aquila sí non li s'affisse unquanco* (Gazing, as never eagle fix'd his ken). Beatrice's behaviour exemplifies the nature of celestial experience. And Beatrice, *donna angelicata* (angel-like woman), is obviously symbolic of faith: vision and knowledge of the Absolute.

5. Vv. 49-85 describe the beginning of Dante's flight through the heavenly spheres. The experience of the journey is rendered in terms of ever-increasing light and vision. Here the poet aims at suggesting the meaning of mystical vision and intuitive contemplation. The presence of God is expressed and felt as the immediate, immaterial all-pervasiveness of light. Dante, once again, confesses his inability to explain, in human terms, the experience of *trasumanar* (transhuman change).

6. The remaining part of the canto deals with Beatrice's scholastic explanation of Dante's experience as the activity of moving towards, being attracted by and being unified with the *summum bonum* which is also the *summum pulchrum*. The dialogue would seem to be articulated not through words; the interaction between Dante and Beatrice seems rather to occur through the medium of sight and the eyes, smiling, that are as mirrors of divine light.

We can now attempt a closer analysis and a more detailed comment of the canto, following the suggested division outlined above.

> *La gloria di colui che tutto move*
> *per l'universo penetra e risplende*
> *in una parte piu e meno altrove.* (1-3)

(His glory, by whose might all things are moved, pierces the universe and in one part sheds more resplendence, elsewhere less).

In *Paradiso* we are in the presence of God. And God's essence is expressed in the first word: *la gloria*. Glory means splendour, triumphant, superabounding, self-effusive light. God's eternal, luminous presence is active in the whole universe, though in different degrees of self-participation and transparency. Divine glory pierces, permeates and constitutes the entire universe and the essence of each individual being, and at the same time it is active and manifests itself by shining to a greater or lesser degree.[4] God's luminous, purely spiritual essence is infinitely active in *moving all*. This is the conception of the Absolute as first principle, source and cause of the universe: the creator and First Mover. To be precise, there is no reference, in the first verses, to the idea of God as creator. We find, rather, a suggestion of and reference to the Greek and pagan tradition. For Aristotle, the *Nous*, the pure, divine intellect, *moves by being loved*. For Plato, the supreme idea, the *kaloagathia*, the most loved, is pure luminosity, the final source of intelligibility and visibility, or presence, in being.

The glory of the Prime Mover moves the celestial spheres, attracts the souls of the *beati*, orders the whole universe, pre-ordains man's spiritual faculties, and finally satisfies them through the dialectics of knowledge, love, aesthetic and mystical contemplation.[5]

2. Here, Dante tells us that he has been in the supreme heavenly sphere, the immobile *Empireo*, the seat of God and hence the cosmological place which enjoys most light. Note the *I was* (*fu'io*). It could be interpreted as a perfect tense, thus suggesting a fulfilled experience. I would venture to suggest that the *fu'io* could be read as a Greek *aorist* expressing an unlimited, inexhaustible mode of action, a-temporal and beyond time. And, indeed, the poet is urged to confess his inability to recount what he saw. To recount presupposes the memory of past experience, and memory can retain the discursive, temporally articulated succession of things and events only if these are the object of physical experience. According to Medieval theories of knowledge, only the material object is the adequate object of human knowledge, understanding and memory; only the physical object primarily, and what can be abstracted therefrom, can be analysed discursively (step by step, through *reasoning*, in a mediated fashion) and hence remembered.[6]

Dante writes the poetry of a super-human experience. The mind, being nearest to the final object of knowledge and love, reaches such hei-
ghts of spiritual illumination that memory fades and fails. In other
words, the paradisiac experience exceeds the bounds of our quotidian
and imperfect fashion of knowing through the senses in a laboriously
discursive manner by means of analogies *(as in a mirror),* and then of
loving the object known to be true and good. Discursive experience sees
and loves God as in a mirror. Through mystical vision, on the contrary,
the Blessed *(beati)* in *Paradiso* (and the poet with them) are gratified by
an intuitive knowledge, an immediate contact of love and, in synthesis,
by the spiritually fulfilled light of contemplation. God is intuitively held
as Truth, Goodness and Beauty, at once.

3. After the theme of mystical and beatific vision, we find it rather
strange and even disconcerting to hear the poet's invocation: *O buono
Apollo* (Benign Apollo). After a brief outline of the Christian conception of the cosmos (even though the idea of God as creator is not mentioned), we are suddenly introduced to the pagan cosmos. This is not the
only time when Dante invokes and makes reference to pagan mythology.
His references are partly inspired by his awareness of the Western cultural heritage and its origins, ancestry and foundations. They are, furthermore, motivated and sustained by the Medieval conviction that poetry, among the *artes,* is a secular occupation and, indeed, one worthy
of a pagan's dedication.

Dante was familiar with Plato's *Phaedrus* and the attractive idea of
divine inspiration as *mania.* And the poet is aware that he needs divine
inspiration for the completion of his divine poem. Apollo is the ancient
God of reason and of poetic vision, the God of light, the sun-god. But
he stands for Christ, the splendour of the Father. Apollo is the god of
the poets' cherished laurel and, at once, the God of the cross. He is the
pagan god *who drew Marsyas from the scabbard of his limbs,* and the
Christian God who is asked to influence the poet, to work on him, as an
artist works on his chosen material.

God has been spoken of as glory, light, prime mover, goal and aim of
our knowledge, love, contemplation. In the context of the poet's invocation, God is also presented as source of poetic inspiration and as
Supreme Artist.

4. The particular configuration of the stars determines the moment in
time when, more readily and more successfully, *la lucerna del*

mondo...la mondana cera / piú a suo modo tempera e suggella (The world's bright lamp...To the worldly wax, best gives / Its temper and impression). Mediated, as it were, by the influence of the stars, God exercises his creative, *artistic,* formative power upon *the worldly wax.* From the astronomical details we understand that it was noon,

> *quando Beatrice in sul sinistro fianco*
> *vidi rivolta a riguardar nel sole:*
> *aquila sí non li s'affisse unquanco.* (46-48)
> (when to the left I saw Beatrice turn'd, and on the sun gazing, as never eagle fix'd his ken).

After a long, detailed, symbolically overloaded description of the position of the constellations, the mention and the very appearance of Beatrice are quite sudden, even unexpected, and determine a significant turning-point in the movement of the canto. After the economical and robust beginning, the hesitant announcement of mystical experience and the relatively tedious (because excessively hermetic) description of the constellations, it seems as if, introducing Beatrice, the poet is at once inspired and imbued with renewed poetic enthusiasm. *Aquila sí non si s'affisse unquanco* (As never eagle fix'd his ken). In this noble, powerful verse, the image of the eagle is particularly effective. This superb flier, this creature of the air can, among the creatures of the earth, gaze into the sun without harm. Furthermore, Beatrice's fixed gaze upon the light determines the beginning of motion, the flight towards higher spheres. Seeing the light of the sun mirrored in Beatrice's eyes, and participating in Beatrice's mystical contemplation of light, Dante's sight is attracted towards the celestial spheres. The same act of seeing is also the ascending movement of the poet. There is no indication, in the text, that could suggest the experience of physical and spatial motion. Dante only uses images that convey the experience of increasing light: *parve giorno a giorno essere aggiunto...avesse il ciel d'un altro sole adorno.* And this, the realm of light, is the place to which we naturally aspire, designed by Divine Providence, as the very goal of our human existence.

A new reference to Beatrice introduces a more cogent treatment of mystical experience:

> *Beatrice tutta nell'etterne rote*
> *fissa con li occhi stava; ed io in lei*
> *le luci fissi* ...(64-66)
> (Her eyes fast fix'd on the eternal wheels, Beatrice stood unmoved, and I with ken fix'd upon her...)

The poet contemplates, with immobile fixity, through the eyes of faith; and he experiences a transformation within himself, similar to that undergone by Glaucus of pagan mythology. The poet feels as though metamorphosed into something divine and god-like. The reference to Glaucus softens the otherwise apparently blasphemous claim. Anyway, the mystical experience could not be rendered adequately in human language: *trasumanar significar per verba / non si poría* (Words may not tell of that transhuman change). The poet is seized by wonder and doubt, and expresses himself not unlike other mystics, before and after him (Was I with my body? Was I without my body? I do not know. God knows it.), quoting, among others, St. Paul.[7]

Vv. 76-84 gives us a more detailed description of Dante's experience of flight through ever-increasing light: an ocean of light and the harmony of the spheres.[8] The poet wonders at the nature of his flight, and the doubt is perceived by Beatrice, without his asking. *Tu non se' in terra, sí come tu credi* (Thou art not on Earth as thou believest). You are not on Earth! (We note that this is one of the very rare references to earth, in the entire *Paradiso*). And Beatrice continues: *ma folgore fuggendo il proprio sito, / non corse come tu ch'ad esso riedi* (For lighting scaped from its own proper place, / Ne'er ran, as thou hast hither now return'd). The few and brief words are not so much uttered, as smiled. Dante describes them as *sorrise parolette brevi* (Brief words accompanied with smiles). The eloquent smile suspends and supersedes the normal human means of verbal communication. The dialogue between Dante and Beatrice, man and Faith, is a mysterious interaction, not discursively articulated, but intuitively held. The poet must write words, for his readers, but he takes care that the words suggest the immediate quality of an inner dialogue of the soul with itself, of man with God, of the contemplator with the contemplated beauty that is also truth and love, that is light and self-transparency. The poet sees, moves and experiences along a continuous, unbroken flow of energy and activity. In this he renders the motion, the continuity and immateriality of light itself: *la gloria di colui che tutto move* (The glory, by whose might all things are moved).

Dante's further doubt, *ma ora ammiro / com'io trascenda questi corpi lievi* (But now admire / How I above those lighter bodies rise), solicits further explanations and another dialogue, once again introduced and expressed by the movement of Beatrice's eyes, another dialogue made of pure visibility, immediate and intuitive like the very element of *Paradiso,* that is light. And Beatrice's model and form of explanation, circular and intuitive, though articulated as a scholastic syllogism, reproduces and effectively renders the very content of the explanation: the circularity, the order, the participation of all things in the perfection of being and in God's love for the created universe. Beatrice's explanations focus upon the significance of the final cause. The teleology of the entire universe directs and inspires each individual being and each individual faculty or even instinct. Finally it reaches its proper and adequate fulfilment in God as the supreme object of knowledge, love and contemplation.

> *Le cose tutte quante*
> *hanno ordine tra loro, e questo è forma*
> *che l'universo a Dio fa simigliante.* (103-105)
> (Among themselves all things have order; and from hence the form, which makes the universe resemble God).

With these words begins the detailed presentation of the Christian cosmos. The first three verses of the canto are here thematically treated and expanded; furthermore, with Beatrice's explanations, we also have the detailed announcement, the prelude of the entire life, experience and structure of *Paradiso.* The realm of *la gloria di colui che tutto move* (The glory, by whose might all things are moved), is also the universe of undisturbed order and harmony. Order and harmony permeate and illuminate the Christian cosmos, according to different measures of participation in and proximity to eternal light. That proximity is given in degrees of order and intensity of light and transparency. The idea of *order,* as a universal attribute and form of all things, *che l'universo a Dio fa simigliante* (which makes the universe resemble God), is clearly inspired by Platonic and Neo-Platonic sources, even mediated by St. Augustine. The universe *resembles* God in its being ordered, and it strives, furthermore, to achieve an increasingly higher degree of ordered resemblance to God and the final unification with Him. At the apex of the Platonic tradition, Plotinus had suggested a similar metaphysical model of the universe, though strongly marked by pantheistic overtones. Dante, however, prudently avoids the emanative and pantheistic implications of Neo-Platonic doctrines and complements the Platonic conception of the cosmos by foregrounding the Aristotelian (and Thomistic) principle of finality or teleology:

> *Nell 'ordine ch'io dico sono accline*
> *tutte nature*
> *onde si muovono a diversi porti*
> *per lo gran mar dell 'essere* ...(109-113)
> (All natures lean, in this their order, diversity; thus they to different havens are moved on through the vast sea of being...).

The final part of the canto is a sublime eulogy of the Christian cosmos. The lyrical splendour of the poetic diction is perfectly attuned to the lucidly expounded theo-philo-sophical doctrine. Different beings, according to their individual degree of participation in the perfection of God according to their degree of luminous order, fulfil their essence, place themselves in their appointed haven *(porto),* and reach it by following their internal energy, by acting out their *soul* or their instinct *(istinto).* [9] The instinct, the soul, the order, the goal, God, move also spiritual beings and, in particular, human beings *c'hanno intelletto ed amore* (That have intellect and love), in other words *cor gentili* (gentle hearts).[10] Even these are set in motion by the divine bow. We note the parallelism with and the variation on the motif of the God/Apollo transposition. Apollo *saetta* the rays of the sun. Light, divine light, moves *by being loved,* by being *porto / per lo gran mar deli 'essere* (Haven / through the vast sea of being). From verse 127, the idea of motion and the image of the bow and the string, are translated in terms of formal perfection and artistic creativity.

With regard to the general structure of *Paradiso*, and as an introduction to this *cantica,* we should perhaps add a further explanation by way of comment to and elucidation of Dante's vision of Christian cosmology, especially as expressed from verse 121 to the end of the canto. The *immobile Empireo (*immobile Empyrean), the seat of God, is immobile because appeased by God's luminous presence. This contains, next and within it, the *primo mobile* (first moving sphere) which spins more rapidly than all other Heavenly spheres. It is the sphere and heavenly body *c'ha maggior fretta (* that moves more rapidly). Verses 76-79 had mentioned the *Primo mobile* as *la rota che tu sempiterni desiderato* (The wheel which thou dost ever guide,/Being desired). It moves so rapidly because of love and the desire for God. The immobile *Empireo* does not rotate, but, we could say with reference to metaphysics, it is so infinitely active that its infinitely rapid activity determines an immobile state of absolute, static, ecstatic contemplation. Here the final goal is reached. Here the entire universe comes to its rest: gratified by the immediate, intuitive, direct contemplation of its final truth, good and beauty. The *Empireo* is, among other incorporeal celestial bodies, the most purely immaterial, its substance as ethereal as light itself. The divine essence, that is light, *moves by being loved,* illumines and constitutes, by analogy and participation, *le cose tutte quante* (All things), operates as *intenzion dell 'arte* (Art's intention), finally, being contemplated, pacifies and fulfils.

Beatrice, having exhaustively explained the ordered and teleological economy of the Christian cosmos, *quinci rivolse inver lo cielo il viso* (She turn'd toward the Heaven her face). Speaking allegorically, Faith, after intellectual discourse, resumes the disposition of immediate vision and intuitive contemplation.

The entire *Paradiso* is ostensibly orchestrated on the theme of *light.* Light is spiritual, incorporeal, immaterial, metaphysical, simple, pure, active without mediation; it is immediately present, and the source of visibility. Light seemed to Dante, as to Plotinus before him, most apt to symbolise God himself. The souls of the blessed appear to the poet as blobs of light, incandescent sparks in the celestial fire of divine love. The idea of God as light is not particularly original, as we already re- marked. The vigour of Dante's imagination is, however, undeniable. I would submit that Dante's articulation of the theme of light, in *Paradiso,* can be finally interpreted as the poetics of itself. It determines the *all- inclusiveness* or *self-containment* of the *Commedia.* And these are the marks of great poetry. *Paradiso,* with its perfectly beautiful diction, is the poetic treatment of the experience of *contemplatio,* the experience of beauty, the ontology of beauty.

The Bishop of Lincoln and Chancellor of Oxford University, Robert Grosseteste, attempted in his writings an articulation of a metaphysics of light.[11] In the *Hexaemeron,* for instance, he wrote:

> *Lux igitur est pulchritudo et ornatus omnis visibilis creaturae. ... Prima vox Domini naturam luminis fabricavit...Haec per se pul- chra est quia eius natura simplex est, sibique omnia simul. Quapropter maxime unita et ad se per aequalitatem concordissime proportionata. Proportionum autem concordia pulchritudo est.*

> *Quapropter etiam sine corporearum figurarum harmonica proportione ipsa lux pulchra est et visu jocondissima.*[12]

Dante's *Paradiso* is the poetic rendering of the Medieval aesthetics and metaphysics of light, as expressed synthetically in Grosseteste's theoretical attempt at systematisation.

I hope this presentation has not obscured the luminosity of Dante's poetry and wisdom which, after the triumphant announcement of *la gloria di colui che tutto move* (The glory, by whose might all things are moved), lead us through the celestial spheres to the Mystical Rose of cantos Thirty and Thirty One the choir of exultant saints and angels.

The rose I see as the harmonious celebration of light. The flower mirrors the sun. The rose is distilled light, we could say. *And the fire and the rose are one,* as T.S. Eliot put it. In the mystical rose of Dante's invention, angels like bees fly to and fro, from God's throne to the concentric rows, like petals, of beholding souls, carrying the pollen and honey of divine love, peace and warm light.

La gloria di colui che tutto move (The glory, by whose might all things are moved) is beauty, the synthesis of all transcendental perfections, and it is love. It can only be contemplated. Dante admits, repeatedly, his inability to explain the nature of contemplative experience. His poetic discourse aims, finally, at its self-negation. To use the poet's words: *all 'alta fantasia qui mancò possa* (High imagination here lost power). Human imagination loses its power because, finally, the mind is confronted with and overwhelmed by what can only be mystically contemplated (and poetically expressed!): supreme beauty, light and love; in a word: God. The initial *gloria di colui che tutto move* is also the final *amor che move il sole e l'altre stelle* (Love that moves the sun in Heaven and all the stars).

Fellini's Poetics of Memory

*At the end of the day we shall gaze into ourselves
and finally distinguish from what seemed to us to
be real, the only possible reality: that which we
invented.* (Michelangelo)

An analysis of Fellini's poetics may well begin with a reference to one
of the director's last films. *Amarcord* is a dialect form, prevalently
employed in the region of Romagna, of the Italian *mi ricordo.*
Amarcord is not a casual title. It does not only signify and justify the
free, unhindered, uncomplicated flights of the gratuitous imagination
which remembers and recreates the long passed school-days and the
years spent in the *borgo.* In *Amarcord* Fellini remembers his life as an
artist, his previous films, his old and familiar themes, all the visual,
aesthetic and existential preoccupations of the past. In this film all the
aspects of human life already explored and contemplated are seen once
again with eyes of spirit. The cinecamera is to Fellini, more so than to
other directors, the natural extension of his sight. And if it is true that
sight grasps more differences, it is not less true that, through the
cinecamera, Fellini grasps the images of humanity, most diverse and
nonetheless unified in the artist's subjectivity. Fellini's films can
unmistakably be referred back to autobiographical experiences, motifs,
occurrences and preoccupations. Whenever he removes himself, as it
were, from himself and from his memory of himself, then his images
weaken and grow pale, then he fails in the end. This is precisely the ill-
fate which befell *Roma* and *Clowns.*

With reference to *Amarcord*, critics have spoken of lack of
originality, complacency, narcissistic repetitions, *nothing new,* twilight
of the Fellinian muse, tiredness, lack of inspiration, poverty of thematic
ideas.[1] It is doubtless easy to recognise, in this film, old images of
Fellini's visionary world. The abundant tobacconist and the sensual
Volpina remind us of Iris-Susy in *Giulietta degli spiriti,* of saraghina
and Carla in *Otto e mezzo* (8½), of the *negressa* in *Satyricon,* some of
the prostitutes in *Roma.* Gradisca remind us of Anita Ekberg in *La
dolce vita,* of Claudia and Carla in *Otto e mezzo.* They are symbols and

archetypes of sexuality, of femininity at once erotic and maternal. Zio Lallo and his friends, and the schoolboys as their young counterparts, are a clear echo of *Ivitelloni* and of *dolce vita* types. Biscein Pinwheeler reminds us of Fellini's clowns. Another prominent recurrent motif can be seen in the queues of little orphans, all equally dressed with cloaks like wings. We see the aristocracy of the small town, distant (they live upstairs) and bored, like the prince at the Grand Hotel, surrounded by decadence, antiques, First world-war soldiers and bad taste, and like the nabobs or decayed nobility in *La Dolce Vita, Giulietta* and *Roma*. In *Amarcord* we meet again the old familiar motifs of the sea, the square, the countryside, the solitary tree. Innumerable repetitions crowd this film. But it would seem that, insofar as they are memories, they signify not so much a lack of new ideas as *the unity of inspiration* which *is the mark of the true author*.[2]

Memory and the act of remembering is, more than just the specific title of the film under consideration, and more again than the experience which provides the aesthetic, poetic and stylistic resolution of the same film, the thematic key and the foundation of Fellini's work overall. To remember means to interiorise, to absorb subjectively.[3] What is remembered is brought to consciousness, transcended, re-created, transformed, interpreted, purified and pacified. To remember means to abandon the presently held point of view, to see what one saw and how one held past events, finally to bring back to the present the enrichment of experience which the revisited past bestows upon us. Memory is no avaricious tutor. It verifies the value of everyday events and adds to them a perspective wider than the dimension of the *hic et nunc*. In memory time is realised as the synthesis of past and present, as the fluid continuum in which past and present live symbiotically, illumine and interpret each other. The faithful, true memory that brings to the heart of the subject the true heart and mystery of reality, soon turns into nostalgia. One realises, while remembering, that something has been lost of what one recollects. Hence originates the sad disposition of the soul which, while rejoicing of its life in time and in search of the traces of its origins and history, takes cognisance of the fact that something is lost at the very moment in which it has been found. Hence, too, the nostalgia which every act of remembering carries within itself, and the expectation of a future world where all the past should find its definitive verification, where all the significant moments of human existence should be redeemed from time, where everything should recover its primordial taste and value, where "all shall be well and all manner of things shall be well". In the memory, finally, the real and the ideal, the prosaic everydayness and the magic playful dream mix and mingle.

From the point of view of the narrative, of the unfolding of the cinematic action, Fellini makes his films run according to the rhythm of memory. His films are made up of dreams and reality, transformed reality, past time made present, past time metamorphosed by the traces and marks of previous personal experiences. The Fellinian universe, his characters, even though constituting a vast gallery of human *faces*, are reducible, in the last analysis, to the inner life of the man Federico Fellini. Observe how the geography, the topographic space of his films consists of the towns and landscapes of Italy, the only country which Fellini really knows.

Amarcord opens with a luminous scene. Gina hangs white sheets in the sunlight. You do not know where you are. A sort of universal geography. The insinuating, at once soulful, sad and amusingly teasing music leads you, carries you away, giving you the feeling of expanding, widening space. Gina, the prophetic feminity, shouts joyously: *Le mannine*! (the little mannas). The fluff-puffs float like signs and heralds of springtime. The scene suddenly changes: from the house-garden to the town-square. The children, coming from school, re-echo Gina's cry, as if it were a magic word. *Le mannine...*! And suddenly it seems as if all humanity has awakened and entered the cycle of the manifold life. The bells toll. The old man, Guidizio, jumps up into the visual field of the cinecamera and recites his poem which introduces the film and interprets its meaning. "Le mannine are the ghosts of those who fly about. They fly here and there, on the station, on the Grand Hotel, on the cemetery, on the sea where the Germans are now swimming as they do not feel the cold...They fly here and there in circles...They fly, fly, fly...!" While Guidizio recites, the camera comments visually by showing the beautiful square set in romanesque architecture of pure style, the cemetery, the grand-hotel, the pier, the sea. In a very short sequence is born a whole universe of voices, sounds, places and characters. We are situated in a *borgo* placed nowhere, between sea and sky, like a symbol and a token. Later the snow will fall from above. And the peacock shall fly down from the sky, among snow-flakes, and land, for an interminable moment, to the astonished gaze of the boys who forget their games. The peacock shall spread its tail and fill the entire visual field caught by a zooming lens, fill the whole screen, as an epiphany of the divine.

The film begins at springtime. Life begins. Signs come from above. At the ritual celebrations of the bonfire we make acquaintance with the remaining characters and faces which inhabit the *borgo* and take part in the cyclical movement of the comedy of life. The town and square are the stage, the sea, the sky and the countryside, its scenario. All the characters of the universe filtered through memory recite their part, act their part of life. Together they live through the cycle of the seasons, of their festivities, of their celebrations of public events, of their fears, of death. Nothing is hidden.

Titta, our *hero*, goes through the careless and thoughtless school-day adolescence, full of ever new games and inventions, dreams and unsatisfied desires, ever-growing vital instincts not yet controlled. The film is Titta's purgatory where the adolescent passions, which mirror those of grown-up *Vitelloni*, undergo the process of anxious expectations and the embarrassing, humiliating delusions of his youthful and inexperienced age. It is the purgatory of the adolescent imagination which sees the woman with vastly abundant breasts and equally generous rump. The *manifestazione* in honour of a laughable small Mussolini, the Duce's speeches, the shots fired at the bell-tower, the questioning session at the police headquarters and the compulsive ingestion of castor oil. This too is part and parcel of the Italian people's life as remembered by Fellini who, when young, had experienced the war and, even earlier, the ascent of fascism.

Part of the cycle of life is the touchingly human sequence, reminiscent of Dostoyevsky's *The Injured and Insulted,* where the wife waits worried for Aurelio's homecoming and takes loving care of the unfortunate man who, being anti-fascist and therefore suspect, has been compelled to drink castor oil. But even this humiliated and at the same time nearly lyrical sequence finds its resolution in a smile, in the thoughtless comment made by Titta who, stepping into the kitchen where his father is washing, puts his hands to his nose and bursts into a peal of childish laughter, with the words: "What a foul smell, dad..." The father jumps out in a furious attempt to seize Titta, and his same anger is the obvious sign that all is normal and well, once again.

Part of life are the ecstatic brief moments of the miraculous apparition of the Rex, during which the lights of the liner, the music and the confused, mixed, stupefied voices produce an experience of heightened emotion, particularly inspired by Gradisca's face full of tears, wonder and sadness. Nicole Gradisca is, in some respects, the most central figure in the film: symbol of femininity and perhaps symbol of Italy, with her heart *full of feelings,* her wish to have a family of her own, her naive, spontaneous admiration for thc Duce as for the Rex that sails away and soon disappears. (In this a memory too: of Italy seeing her king depart?).

The Rex sequence ends in a sort of ship-wreck effect. One sees the boats of the onlookers, as if through the waves of the sea stirred by the gigantic liner. The following scene is a scene of death, fog and sepulchral silence only interrupted and intensified by the menacing, even though softened, sound of a siren or foghorn. Grandpa comes out through the garden gate and seems to be the only survivor of the catastrophe in which everybody else has been involved: the total disappearance of the *borgo*. Nonno does not know where he is. "But where am I...?" Loses his sense of direction. Thinks that this could be death. Then, Tino's carriage approaches, lugubrious as a funereal coach. Only when Tino speaks, in his familiar lively tone of voice, the spectator may think that, if this is a death-scene, somebody else, besides Nonno, has survived. Nonetheless, further sinister and lugubrious motifs appear in this sequence. The little boy goes to school, walking through funereal and skeletal, leafless trees. The wood has survived a large fire. A lorry passes by, with torn clothes and rugs hanging by its sides: the image of the innumerable lorries upon which starved and defenceless people tried to escape the horrors of war and death. Then, the skeleton of a ship, the threatening sound of the siren-foghorn, a stray dog, compose, with the previous motifs, a deserted, sinister and surrealistic landscape. A white cow appears, frightening and, at once, as one of the few symptoms of life. Life will resume its course, slowly, with the sequence on the terrace of the mysterious Grand Hotel, now closed and deserted. On that same terrace where the grown-up *Vitelloni* spent their gay summer evenings, now the young *Vitelloni* improvise music and dance, and the game of their free dreams, under an Autumn sky and a grey air in which float falling leaves. Life resumes its course and gains speed, under the snow-fall of the *borgo*. The snow, and the same word is the announcement of a promise, disturbs the school-boys intent on insistently stamping their feet on the floor of the cinema, and exorcises the menacing sound of drums and explosions in the film. The boys run out to play and to wonder. The square will be soon a labyrinth in which the desires of the young Titta are lost and where he is threatened by the mysterious, faceless motor-cycle driver. The faceless driver, and his military-like monstrous bike, who appears and suddenly disappears, riding through the town, frightening even the stray dogs, appears to be the metamorphosed and remembered image of the Nazis and of the German military occupants in Italy. More generally, the mysterious rider represents that inexplicable and uncertain, should I say: demonic?, element which is to be found in virtually all films by Fellini. Think of the spastic, deformed child, in the mysterious room in the country farm-house, where a wedding is celebrated, in *La Strada;* the strange repulsive one-eyed fish caught and brought ashore, at the very end of *La Dolce Vita;* the monstrous, large and shapeless fish pulled on board in one of the few luminous scenes of *Satyricon*. Think of Giulietta's menacing spirits and of her dreams in which dead horses, clear symbols of betrayal, frustrated and paralysed sexual life, are brought ashore by the threatening barge. Think of Zampanò's motorbike. Think, finally, of the cattle lying in a pool of blood, torn to pieces and crushed in a road accident. This is the gruesome sight that greets Fellini's, and his troupe's, entry into *Roma*.

In the labyrinth of snow, on the square, the motor-cyclist comes and disappears. The boys, at play, hear the strange sound that comes from above. The peacock flies down from above and fills with wonder the village and the boys who stand there, as if hypnotised, and cannot make one step forward, not even when one of them says: "Shall we catch him?" The peacock, unperturbed, spreads its tail and fills the entire screen; like a symbol of the divine and of untouched transcendence.

> But only in time can the moment in the rose-garden
> The moment in the arbour where the rain beat,
> The moment in the draughty church at smokefall
> Be remembered; involved with past and future.
> Only through time time is conquered.

In *Amacord* life is lived through the cyclical rhythm of time and seasons and the celebrations that crown each season. And time and the season comes from above. The cycle of the games and of the *commedia umana* is harmonised and sustained by the open circularity of remembered time. The circular process of time unfolds itself and invokes the supra-temporal.[4] It conquers and redeems itself. The celebration of Gradisca's wedding in the midst of nowhere, in a solitary countryside, is blessed by the rain and blessed by the new *mannine*. The time of mourning, the funeral is over. The time of wedding comes last. Life begins anew. Life is preserved. Biscein approaches the cinecamera and invites us to leave: "Go home the feast is over, go home!", thus provoking in us an experience of absolute vicinity. Biscein is the clown who knows the joyful mystery of the joyful human comedy. At the wedding banquet we become suddenly aware of the choral and circular structure of the whole film, and of our participation in it. The characters all know each other. They all love each other. They all help each other to grow and to celebrate, chorally, the joyful and the sad moments of life. And we think of Fellini, the artist so humane, constructive, positive, who believes in life, and believes that life is granted, from above, like the *little mannas,* the peacock, the snow, the rain, and the seasons.

The memory contains all the themes of the film: the autobiographical experiences, the history and the traditions of the country, the intimations of the divine. You are placed in a town that seems to enclose the whole of humanity, in which you find yourself at home. The circularity of the total structure, as a mirror of life itself, does not allow one to remove oneself and to behave as a spectator. The spectator is caught...[5] The circular succession of events, sequences and scenes, sometimes perhaps rhapsodic, produces its solution, both aesthetic and stylistic, from within its structure and its motion. Think, for instance, of the parade and celebrations in honour of Mussolini. The teachers, so severe and properly dignified when at school, seem, in this different context, to have suddenly lost any sense of dignity and self-respect. They run like children, full of adolescent enthusiasm. One can only laugh at them. The political parody, Mussolini's little race, a totally unexpected and highly original invention, is succeeded by the earnest declarations shouted by the Duce. These are, in their turn, neutralised by Ciccio Marconi's dream of marrying Aldina in front of a new sort of secularised altar: Mussolini's face made up with flowers, and brought to life by their grotesque movement of his pink-flowery lips. Two picturesque and somewhat bizarre *carabinieri,* exuberantly uniformed, stand on either side like...chandeliers! The series of counterpoints is expertly sustained by the alarming sequence of the tense and unnerving shooting at the bell-tower. The dramatic sequence is followed by a ridiculous and, again, unexpected mishap: the loudspeaker falls down on the square, with a fragile and tinny sound. The exemplified and contrapuntal treatment generates, in itself, a circularity of mirroring and echoing recurrences which animates the texture of the entire film. For it, in itself, is totally and entirely circular. Circular too is human existence suspended, as it were, between sky, sea and earth, and on one beautiful day embodied in a town, somewhere, around an exquisite Romanesque square, ablase with sunlight in the morning and with the flames of the infernal *fogarazza* (bonfire) on that first evening of Spring.

Fellini remembers and, patiently, good-heartedly, understandingly, smiles. The clowns, Biscein, in a Shakespearean and Danteesque manner, reminds us that life is a comedy. We know how insistently recurrent are the themes of the clown and of the circus, in Fellini's films.[6] The clown invokes the motif of the circus. The circus is the circle. In a circling dance are resolved all the previously unsurmountable difficulties of the film director Guido Anselmi/Fellini, and, indeed, in the circle the film itself, *Otto e mezzo,* finds its natural aesthetic solution. The dramatic and saddening story of *Cabiria* is also resolved in the circle of the dance. *Roma* ends with the circling race of the motor-cyclists; and it is as if we were seeing, only now, at the end, the city, and as if we were placed at the very centre of Rome, the city itself spinning around us.

The circular movement overcomes the limitations of stylistically pre-established, formalistic, abstract, and perhaps static solutions. The circular movement, furthermore, guarantees, grants the possibility to overcome the constrictions and limitations imposed by the traditional *plot* and by the novel-like narrative, in cinema. The hero, sole protagonist, can, consequently, disappear. The whole of humanity, chorally, takes the place of the heroic solitary soul, and performs the circular dance of cyclical life, dialectical in its nature, always beginning anew, always reborn anew. This is what Fellini seems to say: that life lives. The circularity of Fellini's films hold together the extraordinary, super-abundant, excessive imagery of this film-director of genius. Only a circular *pattern* could possibly allow, and keep in tune with, the extravagant and over-flowing imagination of this most spontaneously imaginative artist. It may well be that the specific peculiarity of Fellini's art resides precisely in his astonishing capacity to resolve the exuberant richness of his manifold imagery into the aesthetic form, the circle of life, without sacrificing or renouncing even the least significant visual element. Fellini, unlike most, if not all film-directors, produces as if engaged in playful games. Tirelessly he plays with purely visual images, never determined or solicited by literary, philosophical or anyway extrinsic references or motives. His are films of the pure visibility. He creates his films, as a child plays his games mixing and superimposing reality and fantasy, facts and dreams, memories, fears and wishes. Fellini's imagination, though untiring and virtually inexhaustible, in this like a child's playful imagination, knows, unlike the children, the power of memory. Fellini cannot do without anything. He needs everything. And he succeeds in magically transforming everything. The crisis, the *impasse* or block in which Anselmi finds himself, in *Otto e mezzo* , consists precisely in this incapacity to renounce something, to decide for this or that, to limit and determine himself, both in his work and in his private life. He cannot choose between this and that plot, this and that actor and actress, one scene or another, one or other sequence. Likewise, he cannot, and he does not want to, choose between his wife and his mistress, or even among all the women who crowd, in his wishful dream, the delightful sequence of his imaginary harem, which rather expresses very precisely the sort of solution he would envisage: to renounce nothing. Fellini, as an artist, is incapable of renouncing anything. For this reason, perhaps, he lamented his inability to produce a formally compact and well defined, crystalline film. And he expressed, during an interview, perhaps even only condescending to please his interviewer and us, the wish to realise some day such a compact and self-enclosed work.

No specific pattern, but the circle is the figure which holds in its motion all the moments of Fellini's score. In the opening scene of *Otto e mezzo*, Anselmi, having escaped the asphyxiating immobility of the traffic jam in which he is caught, tries to find his liberation by flying away. But he is, again, caught with a rope, by the foot, and is pulled down. Precipitates. The mentioned surrealistic sequences clearly mean to say that one can find no escape, and should not even try to escape, from the circle of life and the responsibilities of art. At the end of the film we observe the scene in which the same cars, blocked and paralysed in the opening scene, move smoothly and speedily, carrying cheerful and noisy passengers, the same of the first scene, to the place where the monstrous space-ship is erected and stands in a flood of light. There, the magician[7] sets in motion the final dance, the circular conclusion, the circus-like final show. In the moving circle the *anima,* the soul, awakens, regains consciousness and life, and Anselmi is redeemed, overcomes the danger of total failure. He starts giving directions, orchestrating the dance, the motion and the harmony of the circles: all his characters and all his ideas. The actors hold each other by the hand and, with the acceleration of the movement, find their right place in the essential rhythm of life and of the art-work. Once again, it is not art that verifies and realises life, but rather life gives truth to art. Fellini's art reveals its true nature to be a celebration of the human life.

Circle, circus and circular movement constitute the stylistic and aesthetic, contentive and formal solutions of Fellini's films. The circle is the circus: image of the perennial playful dance and *joie-de-vivre.* The circle is the perfect form and the perfect movement: the untroubled fluid motion of images, experiences, things. The circle grants the condition of possibility to overcome the constriction of a *closed aesthetics.* The circus-circle is objectively correlated to the clown-figure. Obviously, the clown is not the subject-matter of academic aesthetics.[8] The clown does not obey patterns. He is, at once, sad and cheerful, earnest and playful, always deeply human. The clown is, in himself, a work of art and a prism of the human condition: always on the way. In *La Strada,* a human universe of clowns, Gelsomina, seen as the contrapuntal complement of the brutal Zampanò, is the human, clownesque *anima,* just born, against the animal-like *animus.* Gelsomina behaves like the music of Dante's verses which define precisely the soul: *Esce di man da lui che la vagheggia L'anima fanciulletta che sa nulla, E ridendo e piangendo pargoleggia.* This, the soul, is precisely Gelsomina: easily disposed to sadness and to tears, as to spontaneous and cheerful laughter. The naive, hypersensitive (and not *mad* as some critics like to see Gelsomina) soul, simple of simplicity and not of stupidity; this is Gelsomina. For this reason Gelsomina, *anima fanciulletta, (child soul),* so easily seized by wonder, attracts and charms the children. Children surround her, constantly. Gelsomina discovers in dialogue with the *matto* the meaning of her life, of her being the soul-complement of

115

Zampanò's life. *Il matto* appears to us, in the film, winged like an angel, up in the air, walking lightly and confidently on the tight-rope. *Matto* is the angel, the interpreter of the human destiny, of Gelsomina's destiny. Matto is the mediator, somewhat like the ancient pagan angel, the god Hermes. Thanks to the *matto's* mediation, Gelsomina understands that she must stay with Zampanò The dialogue, their life together, between Gelsomina and Zampanò sets in motin a process of spiritualisation and of spiritual refinement in the big brutal man. It also produces a process of concretion, solidification, realisation in Gelsomina who, with Zampanò, undergoes a process of *embodiment* as it were. When Zampanò kills the *matto*[9], Gelsomina loses her sense of existential orientation, she can no longer relate to the world or to Zampanò who, in his turn, feels remorse, perhaps for the first time in his life. Zampanò feels and, like Gelsomina, no longer knows any orientation or goal. Having finally left Gelsomina, by the white snow, Zampanò appears to us as a metamorphosed, innerly matured being. At his very first show, having just taken Gelsomina with him, he moves in circles. Gelsomina sits on the motor-bike, at the centre of the picture. She is the focal point of perspective. Zampanò gravitates around her; his show is fluid, confident, effective, even harmonious. Gelsomina watches him with great admiration. We see Zampanò again, at his last show in a circus taken by the camera as if it were suspended by sea and sky. This time Zampanò does not move in circles. He goes, head down, to and fro like a beast in a cage. In the evening he gets drunk. He is all alone. Becomes aggressive, attacks a man, is beaten up and kicked about like a miserable dog. He moves toward the sea, collapses on the beach and weeps over his essential solitude. Once the soul is dead, the circle of life is broken down and only the voice of the infinite sea responds to Zampanò's solitude and infelicity. Again, the circle of the clownesque games, the circle of the comedy of life, invokes the infinite. Fellini's films present the ceaseless and inexhaustible games of life. All is lovingly contemplated with a smile and a tear, with a sense of possible terrors and threats, with colourful dreams and magic, with tokens and symbols or realities which may lie beyond time. The remembering imagination, (like childhood, like the subconscious, like the mystery of love that, no matter how crushed, torn and tortured, can be resurrected and lived anew if experienced as an essential life-game) is, at once, magic and nostalgia of the infinite.

To conclude, it may not be all too audacious to propose that Fellini's masterpieces represent a sort of divine comedy in Twentieth century language. One could find sufficient evidence to support such an interpretation. Think of how Fellini's characters are, in his films, transformed, metamorphosed *from inside,* they *mature* without virtually changing in their external behaviour. They are soulful characters, but not psychological entities. They are transparent and diaphanous and tend to realise the ideal of the angelic life, and of salvation.[10] Think of Augusto, in *Il Bidone,* who dies at the edge of the road, watching the simple country women with their children pass by, carrying bundles of sticks on their backs. And the bundles, like Gelsomina's bundles of reeds, in the opening scene of *La Strada,* are a metamorphosis of angel's wings. Angels pass!, singing while they climb the mountain. Augusto dies uttering an almost inaudible: "Wait for me, I'll go with you..." Augusto has gone through his hell of dishonesty and theft; has climbed the purgatorial slope, when deadly wounded and abandoned by his fellows; finally, purged and become more human than he had ever been, he aspires to join the beatified (in their poverty and simplicity) group of women and children with angel's wings. *Satyricon,* with its sunless atmosphere of underground and sewers; with its thick, lurid and greasy smoke which saturates the oppressive lack of space; with its demonic masks, the tortures, the distorted and beastly humanity; with the perennial threats that haunt everybody, as a sort of a devilish punishment and torture of the senses and of the soul; *Satyricon* is the infernal sphere in the visionary universe of Fellini's *commedia.* *Satyricon* is a decayed world, corrupt, sensual and murderous; crowded with horrid human faces always on the point of turning into cruel and frightful beasts. The world of *Satyricon,* which feeds on the most debased forms of carnal pleasures, is not only the masterful visual reconstruction of Petronius's decadent text. More than this, *Satyricon* is the image of hell, where the playful *joie-de-vivre* is missing; where light is absent and children are absent, but when they do appear it is in a grotesquely masked and distorted shape and role. *La Dolce Vita* is, at once, infernal and purgatorial. Fellini's purgatories find their best visual expression in the sequences at the spa, in *Otto e mezzo.* The spa is crowded with silent, speechless and assorted people who, wrapped in white sheets, in the midst of vapours, patiently and in orderly manner climb up and walk down interminable flights of stairs or alternatively, form long queues waiting for their turn to receive from the hands of white-clothed girls (white is the predominant colour at the spa) the glass of salutary water. Anselmi has been sent there by his doctor, so that he may purify himself. At the spa begins the process of purification of his moral, professional and personal responsibilities. At the spa his wife reaches him. And there he has the interview with the cardinal who, from the midst of vapours, without any preamble, addresses Anselmi/Fellini on the matter of his married life. *Otto e mezzo* is, at once the film about an artist threatened by sterility, and about a man who, suffering a crisis of his married life, fails consequently as an artist. (With *Otto e mezzo* Fellini has given the best testimony of human and artistic honesty, he has been *truthful,* and has been rewarded with the accomplishment of a great masterpiece). Think, then, of the confession of the child Guido Anselmi: his purgatory for having seen Saraghina. Think of the infernal confessionals, *à la Bosch,* in which the child kneels, frightened by what he does not know. In *Amarcord* Zio Teo knows his purgatory, in the mental hospital and on the top of a majestic solitary tree. Aurelio and Miranda find their way to salvation, through their loving, even when troubled, family life. Giulietta knows her *purgatorio,* the painful process of liberation from the tyranny of her evil spirits. The liberation comes only after she has suffered the knowledge of her husband's infidelity, and the final silent loss of him. Giulietta must also free herself, purge herself, of the pseudo-religious purgatorial experiences imposed upon her while still of tender age. Fellini builds up his purgatories, as worlds of magic and memory. By remembering he finds the true purified sense of reality. By dreaming, he proves the futility of dreams which become, on the other hand, extremely precious if they help to illuminate the true face of reality. Perhaps even Titta's moment of fun with the abundant tobacconist, constitutes a purgatorial experience. On the wall of the shop, against which Titta lies, exhausted after his heavy exertions, hangs a banal picture of Dante Alighieri. But the divine poet is there represented deprived of the upper part of his skull. And one can see the design of a section of the brain. Fellini is telling us that his film, *Amarcord,* this human comedy, is Dantesque in inspiration, but that, in the end, the artist proved to be but a brainless Dante, if anything at all.

The *Paradiso,* or at least the antechamber to paradise, is introduced by the clown. One may gain access to it, not through art, but through the circle of life; because it is by living that one discovers the eternal in life: the positive, choral, edifying and precious sense of life. Such a discovery can be experienced only living and playing, like clowns, like children, like the *anima fanciulletta:* Gelsomina and Cabiria, Giulietta, *il matto* and Augusto, all the characters in *Amarcord* and in *Otto e mezzo*. Life is a circle, complete in its eternal motion. The salvation consist in jumping into the circle, in abandoning oneself to the joy of its dance; in letting the soul go through all the stages of its purification, as through the *cantos* of a divine comedy. Because life is a divine comedy. Because the divine is not at the end of the world, but in the festivity of being: even if the feast were only a *dolce vita* party, at the end of which, wandering on a beach, you see again an angel-girl calling from the other bank of a river, where the river meets the sea.

The Tree of the Wooden Clogs

The tree of silence bears the fruit of peace.

The title: *L'albero degli zoccoli,* when I first heard it, sounded to me mysteriously and subtly reminiscent of an expression, an image or an experience, I could not say what precisely, obscurely already known. The film had been recommended, in rather economical and discreet terms, by friends who have better eyes. I was told that I would enjoy it very much, and that the film dealt with the life of Italian peasants, *i contadini*. I particularly appreciated the brevity of the introduction, as it proved, in the end, that not all film-goers are *blind* ! My only intent, in this brief chapter, is to reconstruct the motion, the flow and quality of images, the *action* gathered and unfolded in this aesthetic message which can only be called a beautiful masterpiece. The film is made of excellent stuff, and made superbly. The manner of cinematic treatment adequately manifests the map of the plot or the contentive discourse, by convincingly suggesting an organic coincidence between the two. The action is well achieved. Image and meaning are one, like the rose and the fire in the lingering memory of other quartets.

The film introduces us to the epiphanic moment, it opens with six atomic, individual and static, because ecstatic, pictures of a countryside in twilight and veiled by diaphanous lifting fog. The virtually imperceptible, slow motion of the cinecamera only emphasises and foregrounds the serene nobility of the imaginary universe we are approaching and entering. The images introduce us to a well-cared-for, well-ordered cosmos: the neatly tilled land (and we already sense the fatigue, the toil and the presence of the human hand); the well disposed lines of mulberry trees (they are not poplars as some critics have suggested!); the wooden bridge, that tells you of home, across peaceful, murmuring waters; the farmstead asleep, set in its ordered surrounding landscape (for the farmstead is the gravitational centre of this gently softly an-

120

nounced universe). Against the background of this image we read the caption, which is also the first clue to the understanding of the plot:

> A farmstead in Lombardy, at the end of the last century, would have looked like this. Four or five families of peasants would have lived in it...The house, the stables, the land, the trees, part of the animals and of the tools belonged to the *padrone,* and two thirds of the harvest were due to him.

The explanatory caption informs us and, at once, stimulates our attention, by introducing a discordant note, if ever so gently. Then we see the bridge again, but from a closer distance and with approaching eyes (the camera slowly zooms up close-by, and we anticipate future encounters with the bridge and its peaceful waters); finally, the picture of the bell-tower above the roofs of a small village.

The light increases and the candles are snuffed, with ritual, patient movement, upon the altar. From the interior of the church, after service, we are taken into the sacristy. The parish priest, taking off his robes, talks to a couple of peasants. I think it justifiable, and indeed necessary, to reconstruct that dialogue, for the couple (and the woman is with child) will be, after this precise moment in the sacristy, the nearest to the *tree.*

The dialogue is essentially spare, dignified, as though articulated in a sacred language. Lingering, thoughtful silences bind together, they do not divide, the few sentences exchanged between the priest and Batistí. (Should I be so boring as to mention that, insofar as in every well-construed model or message nothing is irrelevant or dispensable, and every detail has its own meaning, the name Batistí was intentionally chosen?) This man will prove to be, in the end, a fore-runner, like the baptist of biblical memory, an explorer and the prophet of a possible new manner of things, a probable new order of things. Don Carlo, in his unpolished, unaffected and trusted wisdom, tells Batistí of his child Minek: "That one is a boy who ought to go to school". Batistí can only comment: "Six kilometers to go and six to come back, they seem a little too much". Of course, Batistí would be concerned with the hardship to be met by his little child, his eldest, if he were to go to school. They live in the last decade of the Nineteenth century, and in Lombardy where the winters are hard and lasting. Don Carlo reassures Batistí: "Minek is young and has good legs". The following remark by Batistí and Don Carlo's final statement grant us an initial understanding of the plot and, more so, of the film's action. The peasant is poor, he needs help to work the land he does not even own. "He (Minek) could have started to help me". And Don Carlo answers: "If he does not help you now, he will help you when he is grown-up". Then he soon adds, in his country dialect: "meanwhile, let the providence do its work". The final remark suggests what is perhaps the main theme of the entire film: "If our *Lord* has given your son intelligence, this is the sign that He expects from him more than from any other children. And our duty is to respect and follow the will of our *Lord* ".

Batistí is, of course, perplexed. On the way home, with his wife, he mutters: "This sort of worry is all I needed!...The son of peasants going to school!" Peasants are poor and own little, very little, so they need their children to help in the fields; hence they cannot afford to send their children to school. But, furthermore, peasants are peasants and they are not even supposed to be educated. This is how Batistí thinks. And perhaps he is right. But, then, he is a Christian and a religious soul. He must, therefore, respect and follow the Lord's will. Minek has been given intelligence. His parents will send him to school. With ritually tender care, the mother stitches a humble piece of cloth turning it into a school satchel: a new, unfamiliar and indeed improbable artefact among the tools and utensils of the peasant's life. Batistí asks his son: "Are you happy to go to school?" The answer comes in the image of two big, beautiful, innocent eyes, timidly smiling at us from the screen. The peasant's life is a world of innocence. With pride and apprehension, Batistí follows Minek's departure from the farmstead towards learning and knowledge: a world from which he had been precluded.

Life unfolds in the farmstead, the life of five families. They gather the harvest together on a sunny morning in late summer; they process the maize, singing, on a sunny afternoon and, at evening, in one of their store-rooms, reciting the rosary. The children play, work and listen. The adults delight in the celebration of the harvest: a celebration of dignified labour. And we, the spectators, are absorbed and attracted by this universe of unfamiliar values. Or are we not perhaps attracted by the ancestral memory of that existence? After all, all cultures have begun with the ordering of the land and the ritual celebration of seasonal toil. After all, all of us can claim, through ascendancy, a link with the land and a form of existence not unlike that of Olmi's peasants. Doubtless we all belong to a tree, perhaps not too unlike the tree in Olmi's film.

We are caught in a universe, splendidly manifested by Olmi's superb treatment of light, colour and photography. The camera moves slowly, almost imperceptibly. Mostly it moves *towards* the chosen object, rather than across its face, vertically or horizontally. And this treatment, if my observation is correct, renders us totally unaware of the presumed existence of the camera, director, crew and all the tricks of the trade. This aesthetic contrivance, furthermore, allows us to immerse ourselves in the relatively static wide scenarios, undisturbed, as it were, by the awareness that somebody else sees instead of and before ourselves. It also grants us the experience of proximity with the seen object: we move towards it, until it stops being an *object*. Images, a face, a hand, a satchel, a bridge, a stream, or even emotional and mental processes, are immediately, intuitively grasped. They delight us for the arresting energy they luminously manifest. You see and you are delighted, at once. If, however, my previous observation is not correct, I still think that Olmi succeeds, in this film, in making himself discreetly unnoticed. The key-tone and the total aura of this film is its softness, gentleness, respectful care. These qualities adequately harmonise with the patience, the strength, the dignity, the simple nobility of the characters, in the film, and of their lived experience. The laborious, innocent and frugal life of the peasants is celebrated, perhaps even sentimentally beautified, by the quality of the colour and the light, and by the composition of some scenes reminiscent of painters like Fattori and perhaps even Millet. The nobility of the *vita contadina* is formally underlined and foregrounded by the slow motion of the camera. We are absorbed into a self-contained, un-distracted, self-sufficient universe. Even the musical comment emphasises this character of self-sufficient inwardness. The tolling of the church-bells and Bach's adagios effectively remind us and indeed convince us of the topographic and spiritual self-inclusive totality of the portrayed experience. But I would, furthermore, suggest that the self-inclusive totality of this universe is particularly achieved, as aesthetic solution, by the quality of the *word*. The dialogue, through the entire film, is almost absent. The word is sparingly employed and uttered with gentle modesty, with humility. This essential quality of the dialogue heightens the aesthetic experience of measured *retention:* not one *word* too many!

Olmi is not trying to be fashionable, and is not trying to be *spectacular* or *impressive. The Tree of the Wooden Clogs* is as different and removed from Bertolucci's *1900* as, suggesting a wild analogy, Bergman's *Shame* is different from *Apocalypse Now* or, if you please, Fellini's *La Dolce Vita* is different, to say the least, from Sjoman's boring, unconvincing and castrated *Taboo* !

I said before that Olmi succeeds in making himself, as director, virtually unnoticed. I would now add that all the characters, as indeed all the ingredients, in the film behave according to the same instinct of modesty. They act the *silence* that nourishes their spiritual identity and substance. The final result is a wonderful experience of delicate gentleness and peaceful contemplation.

The cinematic plot unfolds according to the sequence of the seasons, a self-enclosed, circular rhythm of time, and the metamorphoses of the perennial land. The seasons and the land orchestrate and harmonise the human world of the peasants; they link together, they bind the different characters, their individual existence and the different incidents. All ages of life, and diverse dispositions, are enacted and, by and large, only the best and most noble features of each age and disposition are highlighted. The weaker attributes, for even these make up the *stuff* of human existence, are treated with gentle humour. Think, for instance, of Finard easily angered by his grown-up son. Finard is the only character who indulges in outbursts of temperamental aggressiveness. It is, in the end, a mild and innocent form of aggressiveness. In one case, the son has the better hand and manages to restrain the father, thus angering him even more. In another case, the horse, with the golden coin entrusted to its hoof and lost, accused of theft and beaten by Finard, retaliates and charges the man, pursuing him around the farmyard and cornering him in the stable. The man is rescued by his friends and is confined to his bed (ranting and raving: "that horse is a thief!"), until the *wise woman* is called to perform her healing office: an amusing trick of witchcraft. Think of *nonno* Anselmo who, secretively, during the night of the first snow-fall, goes out to manure the small plot of ground where he will grow his premature tomatoes. Think of his loving care and the touching dialogues he entertains with his grand-niece, explaining to her his secret strategy and suggesting the secret and mysterious alchemy of the land and of the growth in nature. Nonno Anselmo, of course, is a wise man. In point of fact, all citizens of this innocent universe are equally wise and wholesome. Because they are peasants and because they are religious peasants. They don't fail to recite their rosary at the end of the day and to say grace at meal-times, they don't fail to be charitable to the unfortunate beggar even though their meal is far from generous and abundant, they go to mass, they respect their priest, they believe in the sacraments, they believe in miracles and they trust in providence. Illiterate and poor as they are, they already belong to the kingdom of Heaven. Their sincere, innocent, deep religious feelings, touchingly convincing as they are, turn their humble universe into a sacred cosmos. Think of the poor widow Runk who imploringly prays that her cow be saved from prognosed death. A bottle of water from the stream near the chapel cures the animal. The washer-woman has asked for a miracle. She believes she has been granted one. So, obviously these peasants are exceptionally good christians. But they are peasants, nonetheless. And I think that Olmi has created this universe imbued with religious inspiration and sacred pathos, because he has brought to light the nobility of self-respecting and dignified existence through the prism of religious and christian values. At once, Olmi has presented religious faith and christianity through and within the prism of peasant life: the vital contact with mother earth. Think of the touching sequence when the widow's eldest son affirms the consciousness of the dignity that belongs to him and to the members of his family. The younger brother and sister will not go to a charitable institution, because he can, as he must, look after them. As expression of courage, dignity and loving care, he tells his mother: "They will not go anywhere. We will stay together as a family, so long as I am here to work and provide for the younger ones". The brief dialogue with the mother is another significant example of Olmi's tactful, well measured, essentially economical and effective strategy.

The most elaborately spun thread of the entire plot begins one evening of late Autumn, along a path through the fields. Timidly, modestly, most delicately, Olmi invents the love story of Stefano and Maddalena. The initial tension of the sequence (a man pursuing a young lady through deserted fields) is diffused in the astonished, brief exchange of greetings. We even find the touching shyness of the couple quite amusing. Stefano: "I only wish to bid you good evening"...Silence...Stefano, again: "And you, have you nothing to tell me?". Maddelana: "Well, then, I also bid you good evening"; and she walks away. (I note that the peasants address each other with the respectful *voi*). Their brief encounter is carefully witnessed by Maddalena's father. Their modesty is part of a ritual pattern of behaviour. Timidly, and again quite amusingly, Stefano makes his official appearance, with the suitors, at the farmstead, joining the community at work in the stable. They seem unnoticed by the residents. They do not utter a word. Only a few modest and furtive glances are exchanged, for a whole winter, between Stefano and Maddelana. Even after the wedding, the love of these two people does not need words or excessive expression. The idyll is crowned by the amusing scenes in the convent: the bridal couple dining amidst nuns, watching dozens of little children in the orphanage, going to sleep in a dormitory of the convent (were the nuns going to sleep in the same dormitory?) where two beds had been tied together. And finally the couple leaves, having been convinced to take home one of the orphans. A sequence of love. And, once again a sequence treated with skilful touch, by effectively, but moderately, employing humour and even a little irony.

Minek has, meanwhile, broken one of his clogs. That same morning a baby brother has come into the world, welcomed by the mother and by her faith in providence. At dusk, Batistí takes his axe and wraps himself in his cloak. And then we meet the bridge again, being crossed by Batistí's tapping clogs. The man cuts down a young tree, along the stream. Back at home, in counterpoint to the recitation of the rosary and to Bach's penetrating adagio (the volume of the music slowly increasing), Batistí works at the transformation of the tree into the tool of enlightenment. With precise, controlled and purposeful motion, the man makes new clogs for Minek, so that the child may acquire knowledge and be free. In Spring, the violation of the tree is discovered. The trees belong to the landlord, we were warned from the very beginning. The violation is punished with expulsion from the land. Batistí leaves the farmstead, with his family and his few belongings on a cart. Minek's big, beautiful, innocent eyes are full of tears. The other peasants, silent, frightened, horrified, witness the departure.

Here ends this presentation as part of my partial reading of what I have called a beautiful masterpiece. Olmi's peasants may probably be somewhere, now, re-enacting on a screen, the essential act of cathartic liberation, on behalf of their spectators. For my part, I have partially explained to myself what so fascinated and intrigued me about the title of the film, at first, and then about the film itself. The film is built on a *conceit*. The tree is reminiscent of the mythical tree, the forbidden tree of knowledge. The fruit is forbidden. The fruit of Olmi's tree is a pair of clogs that carry your feet to freedom. The violated tree of the clogs, in the end, did not lead to liberation but rather to homeless exile (Or is perhaps freedom a form of homeless exile?). And, as spectators acting/experiencing with the peasants who stay behind and witness the departure of Batistí (a new prophet and new Adam) and his family, we are suddenly awakened to the tragic meaning of the whole *action*. Batistí has knowingly violated the tree because of his obedience to the will of the Lord. He has acted unknowingly as a peasant for too long accustomed to labour for a master and landlord, since he was told that "it is our duty to respect and follow the will of the Lord". Hence the tragic nature of the action. Hence, also, the conceit.

The tragic nature of the action consists in the fact that neither Batistí nor the *padrone* or his bailiff is right or wrong, intentionally good or evil. It is by fate, call it culture or history, if you wish, that Batistí happens to be a christian and a peasant. He has to choose between his peasant's instinct, respectful of his landlord's property, and his religious instinct which obliges him to comply with the Lord's higher expectations of his son, Minek.

The conceit should also be so obvious. Formally, through visual images, Olmi builds his film on two irreconcilable metaphors: the representation of serene, gentle, innocent and noble happiness in a self-enclosed, harmonious universe; and the image of a softly portrayed nocturnal departure that cruelly leads towards uncertainty, the unknown, or perhaps towards a clearly foreseen state of misery, hunger and even death.

I think even Brecht would have approved of Olmi's aesthetic solution. Olmi, in fact, entertains us and gives us much visual delight. The film runs for three hours, but at no time are we permitted to get bored! At the end, however, Olmi allows us to formulate the problem, and he compels us, by *estrangement*, to see the social and cultural relevance of the tragic action, hence to look for an authentic possible answer.

What still intrigues me now, and leaves me quite perplexed, is the question of a future, probable knowledge: a word, an image or an experience which would help me see whether one can defy one master-lord-*padrone*, cut down his tree, to allow the children to be free, only because of another master, lord and *padrone*.

And this is not a pre-historic or a pre-enlightenment question!

The Game of the Name the Rose Plays

Die Ros' ist ohn' Warum, sie blühet, weil sie blühet,
Sie acht't nicht ihrer selbst, fragt nicht, ob man sie siehet.
(Angelus Silesius)

The Name of the Rose is one of the most interesting, attractive, exciting and gratifying books I have ever read and re-read. To date I still peruse at random its pages, never deluded or frustrated in my expectations of finding well-wrought sentences, subtle humour, lucid instances of rhetorical devices, philosophical ideas and comments, examples of medieval thought-processes, prejudices and cultural reconstructions, clarifications and echoes of the author's investigations in philosophy, aesthetics, semiotics, literary theory, criticism. This is one of the few books I would have with me, if any allowed, on the hypothetical desert island not yet touched by useless information and unchecked noise!

The title engagingly intrigued me from the very commencement. I knew nothing about the book, when I encountered it. But when, at the beginning of 1981 and on a flight from Rome, I opened it and read the first hundred pages, I could not fail to recognise the customary astuteness, the genial touch of the author and the uncannily aptness of the title. This is a book about names or, if you prefer, about words. It is, more pointedly, a message about signs. In its historical references, it is a book about the signs of an era. Many of the guests at the abbey indulge in the exquisitely medieval habit of reading allegorical, moral and analogical senses in the events that take place in the isolated and self-enclosed citadel. The abbey itself stands as a map of the world. Brother William (of Baskerville of course) investigates by reading and decoding signs in order to discover the causes and agents of murder, initially; finally, to reveal the hidden codes that generate the map of the chaotic cosmos in which he finds himself. Brother William, in turn, is the sign of William of Ockham, Roger Bacon and Umberto Eco, at once. This is a book about a reconstructed and expanded manuscript: a message penned by the old Adso of Melk, that stands for the events narrated therein. The manuscript itself is about another manuscript and a library. The protagonist of the story is really the self-centred, self-sufficient library, and its token sign, an elusive parchment. We could even say that, finally, the protagonist is actually language with its manyfold manifestations.

Ambiguous, cosmic and chaotic, beautifully monstrous, logically absurd is the library: symbol of wisdom, knowledge and enlightenment, and at once jealously guarded by its perfect symmetry and its labyrinthine cryptic paths, also assisted by the obscuring fears of secretive librarians. Obviously, a labyrinthine library must have its blind Jorge. With this Eco pays its debt to the other Borges who, infinitely more enlightened and witty than the fictional monk, has invented the quintessence of library: ambiguous, perfectly ordered and perfectly chaotic. When the secrets of the library and the mystery of the paradigmatic manuscript are finally revealed and violated, the monumental shrine of messages goes up in flames. The final code, discovered, explodes in self-destruction, only to generate, in Adso's recollections and in Eco's novel, renewed productions of signs and messages. In the destiny of the library and of the manuscript on comedy, laughter, humour; as a sign and map of the universe, is also signified the destiny of an era at its end and the dialectical life of history as culture.

The Name of the Rose is a reformulation, transposed onto the level of fictional diction, of Eco's theoretical interests and preoccupations, especially in the form of his authoritative studies in semiotics. Furthermore, the book is also a generous transposition of the author's investigations in Medieval philosophy, aesthetics, theory of literature and of the avant-garde, the world and works of Joyce, Aristotle, poetics, postmodernism. The book bears ample witness to Eco's consummate skills, as a philosopher of language and semiotician. It also provides unmistakable evidence of the author's familiarity with the medieval mind. In a way, the book could be read as a revisitation to a *place* of delighted intellectual explorations.[1] In his *Postille,* Eco has clearly stated: "As I said during an interview, I know the present only through the mediation of television, while I have a direct knowledge of the middle ages", and less ironically in another page: "the Middle Ages are our childhood which we must always revisit in order to perfect anamnesis". The book brings to new light and life this slice of human history, more clearly and convincingly than through examination of historiographical documents. Thus Eco proves the validity of the Aristotelian precept that the probabilities of poetic fiction are more philosophical than so-called factual documentation. The characters of the novel think, speak, act and experience, as monks who lived during that period of the Middle Ages *should have* thought, spoken, acted and experienced.

The Middle Ages, as the book splendidly illustrates, is also aptly chosen because of the passionate, I would venture to say inordinate inclination, as an irresistible prejudice, held by the indwellers of the era towards deciphering worldly phenomena: their deep-rooted connatural conviction that all is but a sign. *Omnis mundi creatura / quasi liber et pictura/ nobis est in speculum.* In the spirit of the poem, manifesto of Medieval sensibility, Adso writes his memoirs. As for Eco, apart from the semiotic adventure and the revisitation of the Middle Ages, its prejudices and its aesthetics, he writes in the spirit of the rose, this most ubiquitous flower in world literature.

To mention but a few instances, the rose as a sign of the vanity of our condition (*Nostrum statum pingit rosa*) [2] figures in the poem by Alanus de Insulis (Alain de Lille). The mystical roselike fireworks, a spectacular rose indeed!, crowns the beatitude of the guests in Dante's *Paradiso.* With the fire there is the rose of Eliot's *Quartets,* redolent of many other roses and rose gardens. A rose blossoms with the early days of the Italian poetry, from the Sicilian school: a fresh, most perfumed flower (*Rosa fresca aulentissima...*), symbol, sign and name of the loved woman. The rose of Juana Ines de la Cruz stands on the frontispiece of Eco's *Postille.* There is the flower of the *Roman de la rose,* but many other roses (always the same, I am sure, in its endless metamorphoses) can be conceived and remembered by the reader.

The title of the book, when I heard it first, reminded me immediately of Gertrude Stein's rose re-encountered in Eco's pages of *Opera aperta.*[3] Concentrically indwelling, organically unfolding, one in its variety and diverse in its unity, perfectly ambiguous, that rose is a perfect paradigm of aesthetic diction. "A rose is a rose is a rose is a rose". Eloquently, through the channel of this verse, Eco introduces us to the poetics of avant-garde. Years later, with his *Name of the Rose* and the games played therein, Eco has granted a concrete experiment in the making of a postmodern work, perhaps the most rewarding also because the most skillfully contrived.

The book is a revisitation of a past epoch and, at once, an interpretation of the Middle Ages and some perennial problems that engage also the contemporary sensibility. In its plot and narrative devices the book revisits, echoes and assembles, with a generous pinch of irony and parody, pre-existing solutions practiced by other writers in other books. Eco's ironical rethinking and, as it were, re-writing past dictions, narrative languages and meta-languages, is conducted with an inexhaustible vein of wit and humour. This is the reason why,being highly informative and very stimulating intellectually, the book is so irresistibly amusing, charming and very pleasing: an eloquent instance of *id quod visum placet* ! (pleasing upon sight when seen). Finally, *The Name of the Rose,* in its endless resources of technical narrative skills,[4] in its ironic delving nostalgically in the past, is a document of refined and sophisticated sensibility. It is a message that makes us think about ourselves. I consider it an educative and edifying book. For what I have said, and for other reasons that cannot be discussed in this limited context, *The Name of the Rose* must be considered an exemplary and convincing document of post-modern poetics. Insofar as postmodern has become a category widely, and often indiscriminately, employed *a tout faire,* I would like to submit, with Eco, as a point of clarification, that "the post-modern answer to modernity and the avant-garde consists in acknowledging that the past, insofar as it cannot be destroyed, for its destruction would lead to silence, must be revisited: with irony, in a manner free of innocence". Through irony, parody, quotation, metalinguistic games, *The Name of the Rose* plays its own games. It tells us how other writers wrote and how other books came to life. It tells us also how narrative diction operates. It tells us how novels should be written. It is a book uninnocently aware of being a message attuned and respondent to other messages. Eco reminds us that books always talk about other books. In the *Name of the Rose,* Eco has mustered his vast theoretical skills to produce, in the end, a book that breaks the barriers separating art, knowledge and the pleasure of reading. Yet another subterfuge of semiosis, another trick of the sign, another game of the rose.

Let us observe the tone and content of the prefatory note about a manuscript. We are suddenly, forcibly and unavoidably absorbed into a game of interplaying specular references, memories, quotations. We find ourselves on the stage of world literature. Among other precursors, and spectacularly effective, Manzoni's *I promessi sposi* invents a pre-existent manuscript; Cervantes, with caustic irony, parodies the fashionable mannerism of disclaiming authorship, hence he contrives the idea of a manuscript for his *Quixote*. Borges has many stories of writers who pen what others had already written, of dreamers who dream what had already been dreamt by others, and so on *ad infinitum* in his libraries labyrinths of mirrors. Adso's *Prologue* is so obviously reminiscent of Mann's first chapter of *Doktor Faustus*. The chronicler Adso reminds us so vividly of the biographer Serenus Zeitblom: You might call them spiritual brothers. Hesse's *Das Glasperlenspiel* is also written as a biography of the Magister Ludi, by the hand of a nameless disciple. Eco has obviously enjoyed immensely playing his game of intertextuality. In our reading, we too come to delight in the recognition that books tell us about other books, and that every story recounts a story already told. The underlying idea of the end of an era is another point where *The Name of the Rose* encounters *Doktor Faustus* and the *Glassbead Game;* not forgetting the comic ironic diction and the distancing mediation of the manuscript and of the biographer. Like Mann, Hesse and Joyce, Manzoni and George Eliot, Eco delights in reconstructing a cultural universe. Like his predecessors, too, he debates the possibility of overcoming the limitations of a waning era. Like Hesse, Eco builds an abbey, reminiscent of Castalia, as a citadel in which other games are played, following the codes of other rituals. Like Joyce, Eco plays his game of total self-exposure and self-explosion of language. *The Name of the Rose* wants to be the book as *Ersatz* of the universe. And it can be this because, finally, it is a book about language and its token sign, the evasive and mysterious manuscript. We find out, in the end, the identity of that manuscript. It is, we are told, Aristotle's second book of the *Poetics,* on comedy. The manuscript is unavoidably burned with the library. But its content is so relevantly all-pervasive in the novel. What a wealth of subtle humour to tell us the story of animosity against laughter! What perfect symmetry of irony! At the end of this journey through semiosis, narrative strategies and inter-textuality, we find ourselves where it all began: with Aristotle's *Poetics*.

The game of the rose is language. The book, after the manuscript naturally!, begins with *the word:* "In the beginning was the word and the word was with God, and the Word was God". Theology and semiotics must have much in common. From the very first day the key idea, the sign as protagonist of the story, makes its appearance. "My good Adso", the master said, "during our whole journey I have been teaching you to recognise the evidence through which the world speaks to us like a great book. Alanus de Insulis said that,

> *omnis mundi creatura*
> *quasi liber et pictura*
> *nobis est in speculum*

and he was thinking of the endless array of symbols with which God, through his creatures, speaks to us of eternal life. But the universe is even more talkative than Alanus thought, and it speaks not only of the ultimate things (which it does always in an obscure fashion) but also of closer things, and then it speaks quite clearly."

As a machine for the purpose of generating interpretations, this book is, to my mind, particularly relevant and successful in subjecting to demythologising criticism, always with elegant irony, wit and subtle humour, dogmatic and ideological *messages* smug in their terroristic certitudes. Think of Jorge's diatribes against laughter, sustained by selectively chosen *auctoritates* and the final reference to the New Testament where, curiously, no mention of laughter ever occurs; and think of the inquisitor's rhetorical (and again ideological) techniques aiming at disfiguring evidence for the sake of authoritarian and terroristic prejudices. Those pages, among others, read like anatomy of folly, further instances of chaos clad in apparent rationality. But Eco is a consummate hand at reading signs. In *The Name of the Rose* he beats the Medievals at their own game. By a collage of Peirce and Wittgenstein, Ockham and Bacon, Borges and Joyce, Aristotle and Eco, herbaria and bestiaria, he invents other voices of the age. Our author is also consummate at drawing signs. Hence we are rewarded by luminous pages like those coined for Vespers of the Fourth Day. "Now, for the events of the abbey I have many fine hypotheses, but there is no evident fact that allows me to say which is best. So, rather than appear foolish afterwards, I renounce seeming clever now. Let me think no more, until tomorrow at least."

I understood at that very moment the master's method of reasoning, and it seemed to me quite alien to that of the philosopher, who reasons by first principles, so that his intellect almost assumes the ways of the divine intellect. I understood that, when he didn't have an answer, William proposed many to himself, very different one from another. I remained puzzled.

"But then..."I ventured to remark, "you are still far from the solution..."

"I am very close to one," William said, "but I don't know which."

"Therefore you don't have a single answer to your questions?"

"Adso, if I did I would teach theology in Paris."

"In Paris do they always have the true answer?"

"Never," William said, "but they are very sure of their errors."

"And you," I said with childish impertinence, "never commit errors?"

"Often ," he answered. "But instead of conceiving only one, I imagine many, so I become the slave of none."

The last apparition of the rose, in the final line of the book, tells us the secret of Eco's wisdom. *Stat rosa pristina nomine, nomina nuda tenemus:* The primordial rose abides in name, and we grasp and hold naked names.

If not written for the ideal reader suffering from the ideal insomnia, *The Name of the Rose* is the perfect alarm-clock to wake the reader from metaphysical slumber.

Art, Beauty, Creativity And Transcendence: Paths To Reconstruction

Philosophy, conceived in its original emergence as the *archaic* and *cosmic* unification of *all in one*, is the map-of-totality.[1] If this statement qualifies the Greek and Classical understanding of philosophy as the search for the *arche* of the *kosmos*, in modern times the metalanguage of philosophy is practised rather as the continuous process of re-modelling the ever-changing landscape of reality. Hence, for us, even the most complete and systematic map cannot but be open to further expansions and renewed outlines. This is so because, if nothing else, every map as every model needs to be read, decoded, transmitted, inter-preted, hence understood and misunderstood in the spirit of faithful infidelity and responsible violence.[2]

Totality, for me here in time, can only be grasped and defined asymptotically, it can only be experienced by approximation. The resulting design or blueprint, the penultimate probable map, the most adequate hypothetical model would then exhibit, in its minutest details, the essential features of open-ness, novelty, change, order and disorder. The map of philosophy may well reveal totality to be a totality of fragments. Reality may be revealed to be the continuous re-ordering of its parts and elements, as in the galactic interaction of constellations: not a static, closed and fixed order, but a living, changing organism preserving its ordered complexity precisely in its striving towards a more serene simplicity.[3] Following and remodelling the order of the universe, the open order of totality, philosophy, as experience, is the exercise of transcending: it is the foretaste of Paradise.

The fragment that follows is only a trace and an indication, a suggestion and a seminal attempt at articulating a discourse on totality. The main intention of the discourse is the search for the meaning of quality. The leading key-word is creativity. The context is language. The guiding co-ordinates for the mapping are derived from reflection on art and its inbuilt poetic logic of transcendence.

135

It is seemingly easy to argue for the generally accepted, almost obvious, quasi-tautological coincidence or even identity of art and creativity. The words are often used as they were semantically interchangeable and coextensive, if only at the level of their connotative functions. The tacit acceptance of the identity and co-relation between the two terms, embedded as it is in our quotidian experience and practice of language, can be partly explained by means of reference to the history of Western thought. We may recollect Plato's image of the demiurge toying with mirrors[4] and Aristotle's poetic/genetic conception of art[5] as the exercise of *bringing something into being*. The Medievals understood the craftsman's and artist's activity as analogously participating in and imitating the very act of divine creation. The idea of art as specifically definable in terms of creativity is, finally, central to Romantic artistic and literary theories, grounded as they are on the corollary idea of *genius*. It ought to be stressed that the Romantic and Idealistic understanding of creativity rests theoretically on the thematised principle of subjectivity. Creativity is the very essence of subjectivity conceived as the agent and the active process of self-alienation, self-unfolding, self-realisation, self-expression. Art itself is, hence, seen as the objectified manifestation of the subject. It should also be noticed that the Romantic/Idealistic suggestions are, by and large, simplistically adopted or superficially rejected as foregone conclusions totally divorced from their speculative and theoretical presuppositions.

While postponing the discussion of the identity between art and creativity, which I shall articulate in the terms of contemporary philosophical preoccupations, I will begin by suggesting that even the metalanguages of aesthetics ought to unfold according to the logic of creativity, and in some cases they do so. The advanced suggestion, however, is tenable only if aesthetics, as a philosophical endeavour, transcends the closures of normative and dogmatic models, and if the problematic separation between aesthetics and poetics, by and large sustained throughout the Western tradition, is finally abandoned.

Most, if not all, aesthetic theories since Baumgarten in modern times, are articulated as normative doctrines. In this they have, I suggest, suffered the fascinating influence of Plato's Idealism. Aesthetic discourse, in the West, has inherited the Platonic and Neo-Platonic prejudice according to which art is understood as the realm of participated form and beauty, where the idea of form and beauty is conceived as a metaphysically transcendent and hypostatically divine paradigm. From this follows the somewhat negativsing absorption of art by a polarised psychology or metaphysics of beauty, dangerously bordering on one-sidedness or perilously abstract generalisation. From this, particularly so with Plato, also follows the corollary that poetry, far from being an autonomous and autarchic articulation of experience, should rather be in function of moral and political education. Art can, on the one hand, be a serious and responsible playing with memories, images and shadows of ideas, in order to perfect attunement to the order of pure and spiritual ideas. In this case art would absolve its prescribed educational, political and moral function, thus surrendering any claim to autonomy. On the other hand, art could be a frivolous and dangerous, though quite gratifying, playing with images, for the purpose of sensory pleasure. We would, in this case, indulge in it by forgetfully betraying our vocation to metaphysical truth. The Platonic and Neo-Platonic tradition reached its maturity, though translated into the language of subjectivity, in Hegel's philosophy where aesthetics is articulated as the science of man-made beauty; and further survived in all the projects that define themselves as theories of beauty. Understood as the philosophy of beauty in opposition to the theory of art, aesthetics preserves the characters of an a-priori science, even when presented as the systematisation of results deductively obtained after historical and critical analysis. Generally speaking aesthetic theories, grounded as they are upon particular conceptual models, presuppose the prejudices endemic to the adopted and pre-elaborated philosophical doctrine. Hence, aesthetics tends to apply categories and concepts dealing with taste and beauty to the experience of art, constraining both art in the making and the understanding/fruition of art within the bounds of a-priori and abstract theoretical models. From such a closed and limited understanding of aesthetics, taken in separation from poetics, derive its inability to adequately deal with contemporary artistic phenomena, and the endless debates, particularly within the Anglo-American positivist and analytical tradition, concerning the validity of judgements of taste and the very possibility of defining art and beauty.[6] Understood, in opposition to poetics, as a reflection on the meaning of beauty, taste and the peculiarity of sensory experience we call aesthetic, philosophical aesthetics is, to quote Nicole Hartmann, bound "to delude and disappoint us". Otherwise, as a normative discipline which operates with pre-established logical models and categories, aesthetics can never grasp and justify the very essence of art as the activity which aims to produce works distinctively characterised by some degree of novelty.

The idea of beauty, which in classical thought is conceived as an ontological, and therefore pre-subjective, pre-psychological, category and an objective property of reality, implies the principle of transcendence: the necessary existence of a supreme Being and a perfect Order, prior to and beyond the realm of contingent beings. Aquinas' reflections on the nature of beauty, as a transcendental property of being[7], are particularly eloquent and expressive of the classical and metaphysical (particularly Platonic) way of thinking.

Beside the enormous influence of Platonic Idealism, quite congenial to the Christian world-view, as the main source of inspiration for aesthetic theories as theories of beauty, Western thought has been informed by the philosophy of Aristotle. Unlike Plato's approach, inherited by the aesthetic tradition inspired by him, Aristotle's considerations on art initiated the articulation of a poetic theory and focused upon the close analysis of artistic/aesthetic artefacts, their internal structure and the processes of artistic production. While Plato gave priority to the concept of beauty, in order to ground a discourse on art. Aristotle "at the beginning of his Poetics put aside the concept of beauty and launched upon the study of art".[8] Aristotle is concerned with the specific nature of the activity that brings to light the particular type of artefacts we call poetic, artistic or aesthetic. In other words, unlike aesthetic theory mainly preoccupied with reflection on the meaning of beauty, Aristotle has grounded the possibility of a poetic theory primarily concerned with the reflection on the meaning of art as a particular way of making artefacts. Hence, his poetics can be read as a form of literate, reflective, theoretically responsible, internal or immanent criticism. Obviously the distinction between aesthetics and poetics, though indicative of mutually exclusive practices, is stressed here mainly for methodological reasons. They should be seen, by now, as complementary approaches which, in their synthesis, would vanquish many misleading confusions and preoccupations caused by mutually exclusive polarisation of interest and stress. In more general terms, the interaction between Platonic and Aristotelian philosophy ought to be revisited in a similar spirit of synthetic reconstruction, in so far as philologically and theoretically possible. Equally so, and in the same spirit of dialectical revision, the complementary inter-dependence and co-habitation of the classical world and the contemporary mind is in need of attention. Failure to note and thematise the symbiosis of "the ancient and the modern" would only revive the misguided preoccupations of the Seventeenth century *querelle des anciennes et des modernes*. Even worse, it would lead to the nihilism, scepticism and cultural dualism which vitiates the strategies of Deconstructivism and the Derridian exclusive, un-dialectical difference of *presence* and *absence*, heralding, with much noise, the penultimate void of pre-structured absence.

I shall, at this stage, suggest a viable, though abstract and schematic, qualification of the meaning of creativity. Creativity is the source, power and disposition to bring into existence or to produce something. That which is brought into existence is, obviously, something new and constitutes a new event. Hence, we could argue that, in a very wide sense, any human action is creative, that any instance of making (techne or poiesis) is originative of something new. However, we categorise, in a more specific and restricted sense, the creative act as that which gives origin to something exceptional and beyond the norm, something more surprising, unexpected and unfamiliar, something improbable, rare and unique, something more ostensibly rich in quality, something unprecedented and novel. In this more specific and not easily definable sense[9], creativity denotes the disposition to determine a quality-leap: the emergence of a totally unfamiliar epochal vision or world-view, the birth of new ways of understanding, the origin of a new episteme, the expression of a novel sensibility, the discovery rich of many meanings and capable of disclosing numerous, new and previously unsuspected paths and patterns of experience. In this more exclusive connotation creativity implies the attitude to assimilate, interpret and re-formulate past experiences while, at once, modelling projects for the future. Creativity is, then, understood in function of the past while, at once, determining the future. It is the activity of renewing the past: reading, interpreting and questioning the order and disorder of the past and of past codes, while, at once, positing new orders, new codes and uttering new messages. I suggest that creativity should be conceived as a function and instance of the hermeneutic experience and of experience seen as the cohabitation of past and future in the present. Thus understood, creativity could be adequately defined as the leap of imagination into the future, the projected anticipation and constitution of the future, the invention and re-cognition of something new: which presupposes the deep and competent assimilation of the past.[10]

In the light of the preceding suggestions, I can now attempt to articulate and justify the analogy and affinity between creativity and art. The clarification of the meaning of art will provide an exemplary instance of the meaning of creativity. Art, in its widest connotation, is a mode of action, more precisely a manner of making and the knowledge of how to proceed in the activity of making. Art is, in other words, the totality of actions and processes aimed at forming, informing and ordering reality: a "transformation into form",[11] with the unavoidable result of inducing, inspiring and sustaining a disposition of contemplation, aesthetic gratification, aesthetic *arrest* as Joyce would put it. Art draws the horizon of human encounters with a previously alien reality, *the earth* which, by the order-giving and formative power of artistic insight and craft, is spiritualised, humanised, thus being transformed into a *world.* [12]

Simply, and assuming the most general meaning of the word, in art and through art we encounter nature and transform it into culture. If this is so, art is an existential modality and disposition which qualifies and specifies human existence as such.[13] It must be noted, furthermore, that the very first act and event of transformation of nature into culture, the primordial and dramatic event which marked the birth of humanity, history and culture, presupposed and, at once, coincided with the invention of the sign, the beginning of language, the establishment of codes: it meant seeing something as something else.[14] The first act of creativity, the invention of signs, defined, instanced and crystallized the very essence of hermeneutic experience and of experience as hermeneutics. The neutral and meaningless pebble is suddenly seen as the flint, the totality of nature is seen and interpreted as culture and is hence *translated*, by the informing hand, into cultural tools and artefacts. The very first act of human creativity, and its first instance, is at once the beginning of the sign-making process, the "linguistic constitution of the world" and the act of interpretation, or the beginning of the hermeneutical experience. The adequate understanding of nature allows the leap of imagination into culture as the constitution of the human world. The understanding of the past is the fundamental and unavoidable *condition of possibility* for any human constructive project. Culture itself, as endless semiosis and as totality of *project,* can be none else but renewed revisitation, anamnesis, co-habitation and symbiosis of past experience seen as something else. The invention of the first sign implies the overcoming of previous codes, as it were, and the obsolescence of previous forms of reading/interpreting/understanding. To be precise, these are, in the invention of the first sign, neither codes nor forms of cognition or volition. What I have referred to as *the previous codes,* challenged and overcome by the invention of the first sign, are rather instances of purely natural, blindly pre-cultural, animal-like *experience*: quasi-codes of an unmediated raw complex of signals and physiological stimuli.

The first act of culturalisation of nature, the birth of the human world, the transformation and transcendence from nature into culture, instanced as it is by the sign-differential-leap and understood as the origin of technical transformations, and hence of art in the strict sense of the word constitutes a *qualitative leap*: an absolutely unprecedented, unfamiliar and new event. The novelty of that primordial experience is guarded, treasured and contained in what we call *Art* or *Fine Art*: the experience of reiterated epiphany, the presence and manifestation of the world seen/perceived/experienced/beheld as if for the first time, in the innocent light of a pristine gaze. The irruption of the epiphanic event, which works of art imply and determine, produces in us a growth and refinement of experience, grounds and projects our future, activates the transcending transformation of reality into its own ideal form.

The consideration, even though brief, of the nature of the work of art as a semiotic phenomenon, could assist in clarifying the meaning of the preceding suggestions. Let us observe, to begin, that although every act of transformation of nature into culture fundamentally affirms itself as generative of existence and as productive of new meaning, hence as creative in the wide sense of the word, a large number of human acts falls prey to *technical reproducibility,* to use Walter Benjamin's pregnant and effective formulation. In these cases, the light of novelty is obscured and almost imperceptible. The artistic artefact, the aesthetic message on the contrary exhibits, more so than any other kind of artefact, the essential characters and the mark of creativity. The work of art violates the norm. It critically questions the previous codes. It constitutes itself as a message carrier of new meanings and generative of new possible and probable codes.[15] However, it must soon be added that the aesthetic message, while questioning and overcoming the previous structured codes of experience, does not totally and exclusively suspend, bracket, ignore and negate them. On the contrary, its very novelty is sustained, nourished and constituted by the dialectical/hermeneutical dialogue and symbiosis with past reinterpreted, reenacted, re-lived codes. Creativity could not be intelligible without reference to tradition. More so, it seems clear to me that novelty is always the fruit of insistence in tradition; and I am equally convinced that revolutions are real, productive and effective or meaningful, in so far as they are authentic fruits of tradition.

Ambiguous, polysemic and *self-referential,* the work of art as aesthetic message is open to a multiplicity of readings which incessantly and indefinitely re-formulate and re-invent new codes and, hence, further possibilities for the emergence of new messages. The entire art-universe is fundamentally the global experience of interpreting old codes, their partial violation perpetrated by new messages, finally the production of new codes, new dictions and new readings. For this reason it can be safely suggested that in art we find one of the most luminous expressions of what we call human creativity, and that art can be seen as expression, image and form of the very essence of human experience as inscribed in the dialectical and hermeneutical circle of cultural/historical rootedness in tradition and existential projection into an ideal future. For the same reason, art, not unlike philosophy, contemplation and prayer, instances the meaning of transcendence as *going beyond* the given, and the need/desire/nostalgia for transcendence as *ideal order.*

It seems obvious that aesthetics, understood as the philosophical metalanguage concerning the meaning of beauty, the justification of judgements of taste and the explanation of the type of sensory/intellectual experience qualified as aesthetic, cannot but *disappoint us* or encourage all kinds of subjectivist, nominalist and *analytic* excesses and confusions, if not sustained by the meta-languages of poetics, understood as the reflection on art: the processes of making aesthetic artefacts and the internal, objective structure, language and logic of the same artefacts. Consequently, aesthetics as philosophy of art and beauty can fulfil its task only in so far as it articulates itself in an indefinite circularity of re-codification of its categories. By changing and re-structuring itself following in this the dynamism and violence of new artistic messages, aesthetics can assist in the understanding of philosophy *simpliciter* and of the possible future paths and projects of philosophy. It would enable us to rethink the Platonic and Greek idea of *eros philosophos* (love as philosopher). The new aesthetics would dispose us to more readily perceive the essence of art as a creative, utopic and transcending energy.

The alchemy of art consists in expanding the horizons of human experience. It consists in refining our ways of relating to the world and of giving meaning to the world. Art makes us realise that the possible, the ideal, the not-yet-real world is as real as what we in our half-awake, everyday existence, commonly hold as real. It makes us conscious of the fact that reality is a dynamic process, a field of forces unfolding in ever new growths of meaning and new more pertinent projects. Art announces what could be dismissed as improbable and incredible in so far as ideal. Finally, art as a creative experience makes us understand the human world as a world of work, production, expression, transformation of nature, sign process, language, action. Art enables us to redeem the deep significance of play, happiness, imagination, hidden and embedded as it is in the humblest act of making. Art helps us to rediscover the transcendent value, the absolute quality, the divine meaning of what we call life and perhaps do not quite yet understand.

Notes

CHAPTER TWO: TOWARDS A DEFINITION OF ART

1. Think of the latin *ars/artes*, and of the Medieval distinction between *artes mechanicae* and *artes liberales*. More fruitfully, think of the Greek concept of *techne*, which polysemically means: to make, to know how to make, artistic making, art-form. Fundamentally, *techne* denotes a *mode of knowledge*. See Aristotle, in particular: *Metaphysica*, 980b—982b; *Ethica Nichomachea*, 1140a 9. Martin Heidegger has, with repeated insistence, stressed the cognitional character of *techne*. See, in particular, "Vom Wesen der Technik", in *Vorträge und Aufsätze* Pfüllingen, 1954. See also *Nietzsche. Ibid.*, 1961 (2 Vols.), vol. 1, pp.192ff.

A comprehensive, even though chronologically limited, documentation of the Greek understanding of *techne* can be found in R. Schaerer, *"Episteme" et "techne". Etude sur les notions de connaissance et d'art d'Homere a Platon.* Macon, 1930. *"Le mot techne se rencontre des les début de la littérature grecque, avec ses deux significations principales: art (science, connaissance, métier)—artifice, ruse".Op.cit.*, p.1.

2. The word *category* is here understood in its original and pregnant meaning: the act of addressing oneself to objects, particularly to persons, at the presence of the community, on the square, *agora,* the meeting place, in order to denounce that aspect of thing or person which had previously been hidden and unknown to the community. See Martin Heidegger, *Sein und Zeit,* par. 9: *"...das kategoreisthai. Das bedeutet zunächst: offentlich anklagen, einem vor allen etwas auf den kopf zusagen".*(This signifies, in the first instance, making a public accusation, taking someone to task for something, in the presence of everyone.)

3. Think of the artistic expressions of the Greek culture, born of a mythological apprehension of reality and grounded upon an organic vision of the world as cosmos. Think of the Medieval art, totally suggestive of God's transcendence and self-revelation, and grounded on the spontaneous consciousness of the world as created and ordered according to the hierarchy of analogous beings. In the modern times art invokes and presupposes, in all its manifestations, the supremacy, autonomy and centrality of the rational subjective experience.

4. We note again that the Greek words *techne* and *poiesis* denote the activity of producing in general, as opposed to the self-producing activity of *physis* on the one hand, and of *psyche* on the other. There is no Greek specific term which may exactly correspond to our modern and specialised concept of art. See again Aristotle and

Heidegger quoted. As to the Medieval concept of *artes*, see R. Assunto, *Die Theorie des Schönen im Mittelalter*. Koln, 1963, pp.18-21.

5. D.R. Brothwell (ed.), *Beyond Aesthetics*. London, 1976, p.19.

6. On the concept of *tool*, see M. Heidegger, *Sein und Zeit*, paragraph 15 et passim.

7. Aristotle in his *Poetica* 1451a 36, states: "Poetry, therefore, is more philosophical and a higher thing than the recounting of historical events (*historia*). For poetry rather expresses the universal, while historiography (*historia*) deals with the particular". In the light of this statement we can understand in a deeper manner, Aristotle's concept of *mimesis* (imitation) and of *praxis* (action). Poetry does not *imitate* the given reality, *what has happened*, for it would then be like *historia*. And *mimesis* does not mean imitation as copy or reproduction. Consequently, *praxis*, which mimesis "imitates", is not action understood as *behaviour*.

8. That art is not reality, if one conceives of reality as *res extensa,* is quite obvious. See, for instance, J.P.Sartre's understanding of the problem when, overemphasising the Cartesian prejudice, he states: "..we can at once formulate the law that the work of art is an unreality", and "the aesthetic object is something *unreal", The Psychology of Imagination*. London, 1950, p.211. Quoted in H. Osborne (ed.), *Aesthetics*. Oxford, 1972, p.32. It would be more fruitful and less confusing to speak of art as *co-reality*. This would translate the Idealist conception of art as *Erscheinung*: appearance and manifestation. See M. Bense, *Aesthetica*. Baden-Baden, 1965.

9. I write *between* in italics, to suggest that the opposites between which art lies and which art synthesises are only abstract reductions and not real opposites, for they are dialectical moments.

10. That art is appearance and not reality was understood by Plato and later by Nietzsche who preferred to say, with different intentions, that art is a lie, illusion and deception.

11. On this point see R. Jakobson, "Closing Statements: Linguistics and Poetics", in T.A. Sebeok (ed.), *Style in Language*. New York, 1960. See also J. Mukarovsky, "Standard Language and Poetic Language" and "The Aesthetics of Language", in P.L. Garvin (ed.), *A Prague School Reader on Aesthetics, Literary Structure, and Style*. Georgetown University Press, 1964, pp.17-69. J. Mukarovsky, "Art as Semiological Fact", in *20th Century Studies*, Dec. 1976, 15/16, pp. 6-11. S. Marcus, "Fifty-Two Oppositions Between Scientific and Poetic Communication", in C. Cherry, (ed.): *Pragmatic Aspects of Human Communication*. Dordrect/Boston, 1974, pp.83-96. G. Della Volpe, *Critica del gusto*. Milano, 1960. See, finally, the comprehensive work by Umberto Eco, *A Theory of Semiotics*. Indiana University Press, 1975; particularly section 37.

12. *The from which* (literal translation from Aristotle's Greek *ex ou*) is what we have

become accustomed to unreflectively call the *potentia* or *matter*. On the Greek understanding of this principle see the splendid pages by Heidegger: "Dell'essere e del concetto della physis. Aristotele, Fisica B 1", in *Il Pensiero*, 1950, pp.235-95. Now in *Wegmarken*, Frankfurt a.M., 1967.

13. The techniques of anti-art Dada provide abundant evidence of the extreme inversions here mentioned. It is indeed significant that the reaction against traditional art should have expressed itself, concretely, as aggressive distortion of the disposition of the materials.

14. See Hegel's *Aesthetik*, part 1, ch. 3.

15. On the applications of the formula O/C: Order/Complexity, see M. Bense, op.cit., pp.57-8, 447-63, et passim, where the author discusses Birkhoff's formula. See G.D. Birkhoff: "Quelques elements mathematiques de l'art", in *Atti del congresso internazionale dei matematici*. Bologna, 1928, pp.315-33.

With concrete reference to some recent experiments in the visual arts one can note that no-one builds skyscrapers in order to wrap them up in plastic sheets, in order then to photograph them and, finally, in order to exhibit them in postcard size! The dis-order and dis-proportion of means-goals-forms denounces precisely the *small idea,* the *idol* and the fetishistic gesture of elevating to the apparent rank of absoluteness what is, in fact, a miserable aspect and side of the *thing* in question.

16. It is a strange and indicative prejudice that according to which we accept, without much questioning, the requirement and the need to be educated in all fields of human experience while, on the contrary, we expect, pretend and claim the right to understanding the world of art at first sight.

CHAPTER THREE: ARISTOTLE'S POETICS AND AESTHETICS

1. On the logically unavoidable and historical coincidence between *subjectivism,* and more precisely *Idealism,* and the emergence of aesthetics, see my, *Presupposti Filosofici dell 'arte Moderna*. Urbino, 1978, pp.75-78.

2. W. Tatarkiewicz, "What is Art? The Problem of Definition Today", *The British Journal of Aesthetics,* 1971, p.139.

3. On the relationship between philosophical conceptions, art and truth, see Chapter 2.

4. "Art is all that we call art". I quote from D. Formaggio, *Arte*. Torino, 1973. I do not wish, however, to suggest that D. Formaggio's formulation is motivated or inspired by *nominalistic* intentions. See also, O. Hanfling(ed.), *Philosophical Aesthetics: An Introduction*. Oxford, 1992. See particularly, pp. 1-40, "The Problem of Definition".

5. *Ethica Nichomachea,* 1140a 10ff.

6. W. Tatarkiewicz, *History of Aesthetics. Vol. 1,* The Hague—Warsaw, 1970, p.139.

7. I shall deal with a re-interpretation of *mimesis* in Chapter 5 of this text.

8. "...from art proceed the things of which the form is in the soul of the artist" *Metaphysica,* 1032b 1.

9. Cf. *Ethica Nichomachea,* 1177b 1.

10. *Politica,* 1281b 10.

11. *Poëtica,* 1451a 36. See also Ibid., 1461b 12: "...it may seem impossible that there should be men such as Zeuxis painted. 'Yes, we say, but the impossible is the higher thing; for the ideal type must surpass the reality'."

12. "The arts either, on the basis of nature, carry things further than nature can, or they mimesise nature." *Physica,* 199a 15.

13. I refer here especially to the extremely lucid paper, of 1934, by J. Mukarovsky: "L'Art comme fait Semiologique", *Actes du Huitième Congrés International de Philosophie à Prague* (Prague, 1936). R. Jakobson, in his *Linguistics and Poetics* of 1960, has reformulated the same thesis or model, while reducing it to a more formal approach.

CHAPTER FOUR: ARISTOTLE ON DICTION AND TRAGEDY

1. See, in particular, M.T. Herrick, "The Fusion of Horatian and Aristotelian Literary Criticism, 1831-1855", *University of Illinois Studies in Language and Literature,* (1950) Vol. XXXIV.

2. Aristotle, *The Poetics. Trans.,* W. Hamilton Fyfe. The Loeb Classic Library, 1973. (1449 a 21 ff.)

3. *Ibid.,* 1449 a 28-30.

4. *Ibid.,* 1449 a 31-35.

5. *Ibid.,* 1450 a 7-10.

6. Of singular interest is the case of Francis Fergusson who, in his otherwise magisterial *The Idea of a Theatre* (Princeton University Press, 1949), fails, to my mind, to fully grasp the meaning of *praxis* and identifies it with the action/acting of the actors on the stage.

7. The bewilderment and confusion induced by the relatively disproportionate amount of pages dedicated to *lexis* is, for most critics, significantly increased by the fact that, on the contrary, *Katharsis* (to which a considerable amount of attention has been paid) is mentioned only twice in the *Poetics.*

8. F. Solmsen, "The Origins and Methods of Aristotle's Poetics", *Classical Quarterly,* (1935) Vol. XXIX, 192-201. D.W. Lucas, *Aristotle's Poetics. Introduction, Commentary and Appendixes.* Oxford, 1968.

9. E. Bignami, *La Poetica di Aristotele e il concetto dell'arte presso gli antichi.* Firenze, 1932.

10. M. Valgimigli, *Aristotele: Poetica*. Bari, 1916. See, by comparison, the shorter version/edition, of 1926, by the same publishers, where the chapters dealing with *lexis* are *suppressed* because, in the words of the commentator: *alla dottrina propriamente estetica meno importano e contribuiscono* (they are less important and they contribute less to a strictly aesthetic doctrine).

11. G.F. Else, *Aristotle's Poetics: The Argument*. Harvard University Press, 1957.

12. *Ibid*, p.567.

13 V. Goldschmidt, *Temps physique et temps tragique chez Aristotle*. Paris, J.Vrin, 1982, p.333.

14. *Poetics, 1450 b 13-15*.

15. K. Svoboda, *L'Esthétique d'Aristote*. Brno, 1927.

16. *Op. cit.*

17. *Ibid.*, p.330 ff., where Goldschmidt, obviously disagreeing with a host of critics who undermined the importance of *lexis*, significantly remarks: *l'étendue matérielle de cette étude* (on lexis) *indique assez la portée qu'il lui reconnaît; autrement dit: le style est, avec la fable, la seule partie qui relève véritablement de l'Art Poetique.*

18. *Poetics,* 1458 a 18 ff. Cf. *Rhetoric,* III 2.

19. T. Todorov, *Théorie de la Litterature*. Paris, 1965, p.97.

20. See in particular, J.P. Vernant, "Tensions and Ambiguities in Greek Tragedy", in G.S Singleton, (ed.), *Interpretation. Theory and Practice*. Baltimore, 1969.

21 U. Eco, *La Struttura Assente*. Milano, 1964, p.63. See also L. Pareyson, *Il Verisimile nella Poetica di Aristotele*. Torino, 1950.

CHAPTER FIVE: ARISTOTLE'S CONCEPT OF *MIMESIS*

1. I refer in particular to the following representative works: M. Dufrenne, *Phénoméologie de l'expérience esthétique*. Paris, 1953. J.P. Sartre, *L'imaginaire*. Paris, 1940. M. Bense, *Aesthetica*. Baden-Baden, 1965. R. Ingarden, *Das literarische Kunstwerk*. Halle, 1931. (Now translated as *The Literary Work of Art*. Evanston, 1973). Idem, *Vom Erkennen des literarischen Kunstwerk*. Tübingen, 1968. (Now translated as *The Cognition of the Literary Work of Art*. Evanston, 1973). R. Kearney, *The Wake of Imagination*. London, Hutchinson, 1988.

2. See U. Eco, *A Theory of Semiotics*. Bloomington, 1976. This work includes a comprehensive bibliography.

3. It would be quite impossible to quote here even a fraction of the critical literature on the topic. I will therefore mention only a few significant studies. H. Koller, *Die Mimesis in der Antike. Nachahmung, Darstellung, Ausdruck*. Berne, 1954. G. Vattimo, *Il concetto di fare in Aristotele*. Torino, 1961. E. Panofsky, *Idea. Ein Beitrag zur Begriffsgeschichte der älteren Kunsttheorie*. Leipzig-Berlin, 1924. Among the

contemporary commentaries on Aristotle's Poetics, I mention S.H. Butcher, Aristotle's *Theory of Poetry and Fine Art.* London 1895. G.F. Else, *Aristotle's Poetics. The Argument.* Harvard Univ. Press, 1957. Among the vast number of studies on aesthetics and the history of aesthetics, I refer to B. Croce, *Estetica.* Bari, 1928 (VIed.); K.E. Gilbert, & H. Kuhn, *A History of Aesthetics.* Indiana Univ. Press, 1939; W. Tatarkiewicz, *History of Aesthetics* (3Vols). The Hague-Paris-Warsaw, 1970-1974.

4. H.G. Gadamer has particularly insisted upon the cognitional or epistemic function of Plato's concept of mimesis. "Imitation, insofar as re-presentation, absolves an eminently cognitional function". It is a form or re-cognition. This is, in minimal terms, the central idea articulated in *Wahrheit und Methode.* Tübingen, 1960, Part I, chapter 2, et passim. (Now translated as *Truth and Method.* New York, 1984). See also, by Gadamer, "Kunst und Nachahmung", in *Kleine Schriften.* Tübingen, 1967, vol.II, pp.16-26. (Now translated as "Art and Imitation", in *The Relevance of the Beautiful.* Cambridge Univ. Press, 1986. In the same volume, edited by R. Bernasconi, see also "Poetry and Mimesis"). The same idea, of imitation as a form of cognition, is to be found in B. Croce's *op.cit.* where he states (my translation): "We have one of the scientifically justified meanings of imitation, when we understand it as representation or intuition of nature, a form of knowledge".

5. On the Platonic conception of art and its essential relation to truth and to the ethical order of the city-state, see also M. Heidegger, *Nietzsche.* Pfullingen, 1961; Vol.I, pp.192ff. Idem, "Platons Begriff von der Wahrheit", in *Wegmarken.* Frankfurt/M, 1967, pp.109-144.

6. See Plato's *Republic,* Bk. III and X.

7. The reference to Plato aims mainly at underlining the radical difference of conclusions reached by Aristotle. Aristotle rejected the theory of ideas as universal and transcendent paradigms of truth, and conceived the truth of being and substance as immanent to being and substance. He could, hence, redeem the concept of mimesis from its Platonic role of an inadequate, dependent and somewhat servile re-producer of supra-sensible principles.

8. G.E. Else, *op.cit.,* p.12, rightly observes: "mimesis, like poiesis, is verbal and active in sense: not *imitations* or even *modes of imitation*, with the translators, but *processes of imitation, imitatings.* The mimetic process is the activity of *poietike* (either *itself* or its species, e.g. *tragodias poiesis.*)" The same has been observed by S.H. Butcher, *op.cit.,* pp.143-4, in particular. E. Panofsky, *op.cit.,* chapters 1 and 2, passim, illustrates, with much evidence, the same point.

9. The concept of mimesis, in the general context of Aristotle's doctrine, was meant to define the essence of all arts/crafts, i.e. of all extrinsic human activities. Nonetheless, the specific thematisation of the same concept as given in the context of the Poetica has

made it to be a key concept for the scientific theory of art. The Aristotelian conception of mimesis contains, in nuce, the reasons for the distinction between useful and fine art. Mimesis is the primary concern of fine art, while the useful arts/crafts aim at producing functional objects and tools.

10. More satisfactory translations of mimesis have already been suggested. Among others, see S.H. Butcher *op. cit.*, pp.142-3: "imitation, in the sense in which Aristotle applies the word to poetry, is thus seen to be equivalent to *producing* or *creating according to a true idea*, which forms part of the definition of art in general". G.F. Else, *op. cit.*, pp.320-22, commenting on lines 1451b 27-33 of the Poetica, suggests: "The upshot of the whole argument is now summed up: 'Hence it is clear from these considerations that the poet should be a maker of his plots rather than his verses'. In translating such a statement it is hard to repress the terms *creator* and *creation*. This is, in fact, of all the passages in the Poetics, the one where the new Aristotelian sense of *imitation* and *poetry* (art of making) appears most luminously (...). A poet, then is an *imitator* in so far as he is a *maker*, viz. of plots. The paradox is obvious. Aristotle has developed and changed the bearing of a concept which originally meant a faithful *copying* of preexistent things, to make it mean a *creation* of things which have never existed or whose existence, if they did exist, is accidental to the poetic process. Copying is after the fact; Aristotle's mimesis creates the fact".

W. Tatarkiewicz, *op. cit.,* Vol.I, pp.142-5, comments:

"Aristotle's idea of mimesis cannot be taken in the literal modern sense of imitation (...). He saw this *imitative* activity as creation an invention of the artist (...). His understanding of imitation, different from that of modern thinkers, had two aspects: mimesis is the representation of reality on the one hand and, on the other, its free expression". See also E. Panofsky, *op. cit.*, chapters 1 and 2. W. Kaufmann, *Tragedy and Philosophy*. New York, 1969, pp.41-8. Finally, not to prolong the list of other interpreters and interpretations, all documented in Else's work, I quote D. Huisman, L'Esthéique. Paris, 1971, pp.20-3: *Une tradition fautive veut qu'Aristote ait déinit l'art l'IMITATION DE LA NATURE. C'ést totalement inexact; Aristote insiste au contraire sur le fait que l'Art êst toujours AU-DESSUS ou AU-DESSOUS de la nature (...). Chez Platon, l'art ést decouverte par reminiscence de connaissances antérieurement acquises par la participation aux idées. Chez Aristote, au contraire, l'art ést PRODUCTION creatrice de formes nouvélles et dont aucune n'à pu être anterieurement connue de celui qui la crée".* For the understanding of imitation in the Renaissance, see F. Ulivi, *L'imitazione nella poetica del Rinascimento*. Milano, 1959. An informative study on the representational arts is the recent work by K.L. Walton, *Mimesis as Make-Believe*. Harvard Univ. Press, 1990.

11. I quote Butcher's translation. With this, I have basically utilised Else's *op.cit.* and

W.H. Fyfe's translation in the Loeb Classical Library.

12. Among other numerous texts, see *De Partibus Animalium*, I, 5; *Rhetorica*, 1371b 4; Poetica, 1447a 13, 1448b 4, 1460b 25ff, 1461b 10ff. At 1460a 27, Aristotle writes: "an impossible but credible thing must always be prefered to an incredible though possible thing".

13. I have utilised H. Rackham's translation of the *Nicomachean Ethics*, in the Loeb Classical Library, 1968.

14. On this point see my essay: "An Interpretation of Aristotle's Concept of the agathon-eudaimonia", *Seminar*, II, 1978, pp.27-9.

15. See C.J De Vogel, "Quelques remarques a propos du premier chapitre de l'Ethique de Nicomaque", in *Autour d'Aristote*. Louvain, 1955, pp.307-23.

16. I have utilised P.H. Wicksteed & F.M. Cornford's translation of *Physica*, in the Loeb Classical Library, 1970.

17. On the problem of *physis* and its relation to *techne*, see M. Heidegger, "Vom Wesen und Begriff der Physis. Aristoteles Physik, B I", *Il Pensiero*. 1958, pp.132-56, 265-86. Now in *Wegmarken*. S.H. Butcher must once again be mentioned for his analyses on the theme. See his *op.cit.*, pp.115-52. See also my, "Aristotle and Hegel on Nature: Some Similarities", *Bulletin of the Hegel Society of Great Britain*, No.26, 1992, pp.13-29.

18. In the light of *Metaphysica*, Bk. Z, particularly chapter III, where Aristotle debates and rejects the understanding of *ousia* (substance) as either universal species or genus, thus rejecting Plato's conception of ideas, we can stress even further our point. *Physis* is the substance of natural beings. Understood as process and activity, and not as genus or universal, *physis* can no longer be conceived as an ideal, static and transcendent paradigm upon which art depends by imitating it. Not a rapport of dependence, but rather of analogy obtains between nature and art.

19. *Physica*, 194a 28ff.

20. *Metaphysica*, 1032b 1.

21. See E. Panofsky, *op.cit.*, "art does not imitate what nature creates, but rather operates in the same manner in which nature creates". See also G. Vattimo: *op.cit.* pp.21-2.

22. Furthermore, it would be inadequate anyway to conceive of a reality as a static complex of static objects. For the ancient Greeks, and for Aristotle in particular, being and reality are not objectified *data,* but they rather constitute a process and the activity of self-revelation.

23. See also *Poëtica,* 1449b 24, 36; 1450a 4; 1450b 3, 24; 1451a 31; 1452a 2; and elsewhere.

24. G.F. Else, in his *op.cit.*, pp.221ff and 241 in particular, seems to suggest a

reduction of *praxis* (action) to the dramatic action or to the representation, on stage, of the plot. This seems to be a rather widespread misconception.

CHAPTER SIX: THE ORIGINALITY OF PLOTINUS' AESTHETICS

1. H.G. Gadamer, "Die Universalität des hermeneutischen Problems", in *Kleine Schriften,* I. Tübingen, 1967, p.106.

2. I find attractive, though in no way original, the feature that goes under the name of *Postmodernism,* namely the sharing in the hermeneutical idea that the past is given to be revisited.

3. Attempts at an aesthetic discourse centred on the idea of beauty are represented by: F.J. Kovach, *Philosophy of Beauty.* University of Oklahoma Press, 1974; and M. Mothersill, *Beauty Restored.* Oxford University Press, 1984; not to mention E. Gilson and J. Maritain, of course.

4. The recent postmodern revival of the *pleasing* in art, though not always convincing, also because conducted in the spirit of ironic parody, may seem to intend to rectify the situation of neglect to which beauty has been relegated.

5. Particularly eloquent and aggressive are the *Manifestos* of Dada (1918) and Futurism (1909).

6. Cf. M. Dufrenne, *Phénoménologie de l'expérience esthétique.* Paris, 1967.

7. Plotinus' teaching so fascinated his Roman followers that the Emperor Gallienus contemplated the plan of a city, in Campania, as a Plotinian *Republica.*

8. In his introduction to *The Enneades.* London, 1969 (1917-30), P. Henry has noted that Plotinus' philosophy leaves no room for and pays no attention to the drama of sin and redemption.

9. *Enneades,* V 1, 4.

10. *Ibid.,* II 9, 2-4; III 8, 3; IV 3, 9.

11. *Ibid.,* IV 8, 4 and 31. Cf. V. Cilento, "Psyche", in *Saggi su Plotino.* Milano, 1973, pp. 63-82.

12. The numerous pages on the value of education and culture are, more than an echo, as some critics have interpreted and assumed, of Hellenic wisdom, a witness to the exquisite refinement of Alexandrian culture in particular, and of Egyptian culture, more extensively.

13. I am not convinced by critics (Hegel among them and perhaps the first of them all) who find Plotinus' (systematic) order as if artificial, only nominal, imposed from without.

14. Interestingly, Plotinus occasionally sounds critical of Aristotle as if suspecting excessive categorising. Equally interestingly, among other Neo-platonist *dividers of being,* the Pseudo-Dionysius conceives the world of being as according to segmented

hierarchies.

15. W. Tatarkiewicz, *History of Aesthetics.* Vol. I. The Hague, Paris, Warsaw, 1970, p.318.

16. See Chapter Five.

17. Cf. E. De Keyser, *La Signification de l'art dans les Ennéades de Plotin,* Louvain, 1955; especially Ch. II on "Le Milieu Artistique", pp. 15-20. Extremely rewarding is the book by F. Bourbon di Petrella, *Il Problema dell'arte e della bellezza in Plotino.* Le Monnier, 1956.

CHAPTER SEVEN: HEGEL'S AESTHETICS AND THE *END OF ART*

1. *Vorlesungen über die Aesthetik* . Frankfurt a.M., Theorie Werkausgabe,1970 Vol. 13, 50-51. In future referred to as: *Aesthetik.* I quote from T.M. Knox's translation: *Aesthetics. Lectures on Fine Art by G.W.F. Hegel* . 2 Vols., Oxford, 1975, pp.30-31. I shall refer to this edition as *Knox.*

2. The same motif of the *separation* or *division* is to be found in F. Schlegel's writings and in Schiller's *On the Aesthetic Education of Man* and *On Naive and Sentimental Poetry*, in particular. These writings were well known to Hegel. This motif is a very common and recurring theme in the literature of Romanticism and previous to Idealism. Variations on the same theme are orchestrated, with reference to Nineteenth century literature, by G. Lukacs in his *The Theory of Novel.*

3. *Aesthetik*, 21; *Knox, 7.*

4. See, in particular, *Aesthetik,* 106-114; *Knox*, 75-82.

5. In a somewhat ambiguous manner Hegel employs the category of *Romantic art* to refer, in different contexts, either to Christian art, i.e. post-classical art in general, or to Romanticism as conventionally understood, i.e. art in his time.

6. Hegel illustrates this point with particular lucidity, by analysing, among other significant artistic phenomena, Cervantes' *Don Quixote.* This work allows him to reflect on the decline and disappearance of the heroic and epic subject.

7. In the postscript and epilogue to his essay: *Der Ursprung des Kunstwerks,* now in the volume *Holzwege* (Frankfurt a.M., 1963, 3rd ed.), Martin Heidegger stresses this precise point: "...since Hegel's lectures in aesthetics...we have seen many new art-works and art-movements arise. Hegel did not mean to deny this possibility." Then Heidegger proposes a question which opens a path to the interpretation of the end of art: "This question however remains: is art still an essential and necessary way in which truth that is decisive for our historical existence happens, or is art no longer of this character?". Quoted from: A. Hofstadter, & R. Kuhns (eds), *Philosophies of Art and Beauty.* New York, 1964.

8. *Aesthetik*, 124; *Knox*, 90.

9. The reliance on the mytho-poetic faculty, the supreme significance of analogical thinking, is expressed by Aristotle in his remark that the greatest thing by far is to have command of metaphor.

10. *Aesthetik*, 24; *Knox*, 10.

11. *Ibid.*, 23-24; *Knox*, 9-10.

12. See K. Harries, "Hegel on the Future of Art", in *The Review of Metaphysics*, XVII (NO. 108, 1974). The author proposes and convincingly illustrates the thesis that Hegel foresaw the advent of an era in which the reflection upon art, and therefore the aesthetic discourse and the science of art, would supersede the experience the experience of art. Reference is made to artistic phenomena in the Twentieth century.

13. *Aesthetik*, 141-142; *Knox*, 102-103.

14. E. Heller, *op.cit.* New York, 1968, 98.

15. Heller, Eliot, Kermode's *Romantic Image*. Fontana Books, 1976, and the entire host of literary critics who have dealt with the problem of *Hamlet*, finally appear to be echoing and reformulating both Schlegel's and Hegel's critical appraisal of the same subject.

16. See P. Gallagher, "The Dissociation of Sensibility", *Third Degree,* Vol. I, No. I (Dublin, 1977) 21-25.

17. *Aesthetik,* 113-114; *Knox*, 81. "The romantic form of art cancels again the completed unification of the Idea and its reality, and reverts, even if in a higher way, to that difference and opposition of the two sides which in symbolic art remained unconquered" (*Aesthetik*, 111; *Knox*, 79).

18. On the same theme, see E. Schiller, *On the Aesthetic Education of Man.* An available English translation has been reprinted by Frederick Ungar (New York, 1974).

19. J. Taminiaux, "La pensée esthétique du jeune Hegel", *Revue Philosophique de Louvain* (May, 1958) 237.

20. Think of the organic culture of Greek and Renaissance cities, as compared to the contemporary planetary *culture*. The former appears to be highly original and characteristic, while the latter, industrially manipulated as it is, seems, in some respects, to thrive on the boring repetition of easily recognisable *clichés*.

21. See K. Harries, *op. cit.* Think of the vast amount of explanations volunteered by contemporary artists, as pseudo-philosophical comments upon their works and their intentions.

22. Hegel's teaching on this point has been treasured and developed by the theorists of the School of Frankfurt and by T.W. Adorno in particular.

23. *Aesthetik,* 90; *Knox*, 66.

24. The quest for harmony and unity is the theme of Hegel's *Phänomenologie* and indeed of his entire philosophy.

25. *Aesthetik*, vol. II (*Werke*, cit., Vol. 14) 221; *Knox* 594. See the whole section entitled: *Die Auflösung der romantischen Kuntsform*.

26. *Aesthetik*, vol. I 303; *Knox*, 233 (My italics).

27. *Ibid.*, 36-37; *Knox* 20. It is quite revealing that music is considered by Hegel to be the lowest of Romantic art-forms.

28. See D. Formaggio, *L'idea di artisticittà*Milano. 1962. Quoted in U. Eco, *La Definizione dell'arte*. Milano, 1972 (2 ed.) 267. See also D. Formaggio, *Arte*. Milano, 1973 115-117 in particular.

29. It seems to me that the pioneering investigations on literature, by the Russian formalists, are motivated and animated by this fundamental intuition. I can only mention their work and the writings of the Prague School. Semiotics proves to be, on this point, the direct heir of both mentioned schools. See also; Ogden & Richards, *The Meaning of Meaning*. London, 1972; E. Panofsky, *Studies in Iconology*. Oxford, 1939; G. Mathieu, "L'abstraction lyrique", *L'Oeil* (April, 1959. Finally, in his introduction to M. Mauss's *Théorie générale de la magie* (Paris, 1950), Lévi-Strauss wrote: "symbols are more real than the things they represent, the signifier precedes and determines the signified".

CHAPTER EIGHT: DR FAUSTUS' MENTOR AND THE DEATH OF ART

1. *Doktor Faustus: das Leben deutschen Tonsetzers Adrian Leverkühn, erzählt von einem Freunde*. 1947. We shall refer to the current Penguin edition.

2. See, G. Lukacs, "The Tragedy of Modern Art", in *Essays on Th. Mann* (London, 1964), E. Heller, *The Ironic German*. London, 1958, 259-285. Idem, "Faustus Verdamnis", in *Die Reise der Kunst ins Innere und andere Essays* (Frankfurt a.M. 1966) 49-52. G. Bergsten, *Th. Mann's Dr Faustus. The Sources and Structure of the Novel*. Chicago & London, 1969, chapters 4,5. E. Schaper, "A Modern Faust: The Novel in the Ironical Key", *Orbis Litterarum* (1965) 176-204; H.R. Jauss, (ed.), *Die nicht mehr schönen Künste*. München, 1968, 414-28; F. Jesi, *Th. Mann*. Firenze, 1972, 83-97.

3. See *Dr Faustus*, chapters XXII & XLVI.

4. The *crisis* can be taken initially, but only initially, to be a "crisis of style, crisis of the novel". On this all commentators agree. But only few recognise the radical, nature of the crisis.

5. The dialectics of genius-sickness is recurrent in Mann's Works: shared with E. Kafka, inspired by Mann's interest in Schopenhauer and Nietzsche.

6. *Die Enstehung des "Doktor Faustus" Roman eines Romans*. 1949. Translated as: *The Genesis of a Novel*. London, 1961.

7. To this regard, even the solid interpretations of an *ironical key* must not be taken as

an encouragement to disregard the earnestness of Mann's intentions and actual thematisation of the novel. Again, the novel is not articulating a stylistic problem. It is, rather, bringing to light the tragic, desperate situation of the contemporary world.

8. Irony seems to prove the best way to face the absurd, and to neutralise or suspend the paradoxical dilemma in which Mann finds himself. Mann, we could repeat: *divinely denies the divine*. If this proposition can characterise Mann's experience, we could then say that the German novelist, like Lucretius, is singing of the end of a world.

9. *Genesis*, 9-10.

10. *Ibid.*, 12, 14, 16.

11. *Ibid.*, 18.

12. *Ibid.*, 23.

13. *Ibid.*, 25.

14. *Ibid.*, 17.

15. *Ibid.*, 28.

16. *Ibid.*, 37.

17. Here Mann gives a sketch of Adorno's life and personality.

18. *Ibid.*, 38.

19. Lukacs, in his essay "The Tragedy of Modern Art", refuses to take it that evil and sterility overcome. He reads in the novel the end of imperialism and of the bourgeoisie. He reads also an encouragement to the proletarian revolution. "Such is the sense and function of Adrian Leverkühn's last tragic insight: '...instead of shrewdly concerning themselves with what is needful on Earth that it may be better there, and discretely doing it, that among men such order shall be established that again for the beautiful work living soil and true harmony be prepared, man playeth the truant and breaketh out in hellish drunkenness; so giveth his soul thereto and cometh among the carrion'. We have quoted these words again because they give clear expression to what is new: the transformation of the real, the economic and social, basis of life as the first step towards the healing of mind and culture, thought and art. Thomas Mann's tragic hero has here found the way which leads to Marx. At least, in his last lucid words he has forsaken his own bedevilled path (the path of bourgeois culture and art) and described the new path which leads to a new *great world*, where a new, popular, great, never-again devilish art will be possible" (97). We could be tempted to read in all this what we might call *optimistic socialism* or *utopia*, the *idée fixe* of which E. Heller speaks, and which he rejects, with the best that Lukacs offers with his interpretation. Heller's criticism of Lukacs (see pp.267-8 of *The ironic German*) sounds to us too much immediate and even sufficiently naive. Not so much because he cannot understand what to Lukacs meant the coincidence between his finishing reading *Dr Faustus* and the condemnation of modern music by the Central Committee of the Communist Party of

Soviet Russia. But because, by paying attention to such an atomic and isolated instance, Heller seems to miss the valid point that Lukacs wants to illustrate in his essay. The entire essay is based on a solid, and to my mind, truthful, interpretation of the novel as tragedy and of tragedy's nature in itself. Lukacs writes: "In Shakespeare's greatest tragedies, *Hamlet, Lear,* the light of a new world gleams in the tragic darkness at the end". (*Op. cit.* 96). At the end of his essay, after having proposed the resolving optimistic perspective of the working-class revolution, Lukacs can repropose the essence of tragedy. "The simple pronouncement of such a perspective is sufficient to relieve the tragedy of its despondency. Thomas Mann sets a full stop to a development of several centuries. But for this reason the epilogue is also a prologue. The tragedy remains, yet from the standpoint it is no more pessimistic than the greatest tragedies of Shakespeare". What is here found and indicated as essential to tragedy is the force of the *bestimmte Negation:* "If however the result is grasped as it is in truth, as determined negation, then immediately a new form is born..." (*Indem dagegen das Resultat, wie es in Wahrheit ist, aufgefasst wird, als bestimmte Negation, so ist damit unmittelbar eine neue Form entsprungen; Hegel. Theorie Werkausgabe,* Suhrkamp, Bd. 3, 74).

20. The *unhappy consciousness* is here understood as according to Hegel's *Phenomenology:* "...the unhappy consciousness is the consciouness of itself as of the doubled and the only contradicting essence", *Theorie Werkausgabe,* Bd. 3, 163.

21. See, among others: Lukacs, *Essays on Thomas Mann*; E. Heller, *op.cit.*; P. Heller, *Dialectics and Nihilism.* University of Massachusetts Press, 1966, 149-226.

22. At paragraph 7 of the *Genesis,* Mann remarks the affinity between Hesse's and his own novel, even though the common "critique of the contemporary civilisation and epoch" is differently articulated. Hesse's criticism is a "Utopian dream-like philosophy of culture, more than...expression of our suffering and recognition of our tragedy".

23. "Colloqui con Kafka" (Milano, 1965). Gustav Janouch records these words pronounced by Kafka in 1920.

24 Adorno's philosophy is received with an ever-increasing interest in English-speaking countries.

25. Adorno's contribution exceeded by far the sole task of clarifying to Mann esoteric features of dodecaphonic composition or of Beethoven's revolutionary innovations. The only writers who to my knowledge, recognise the important role of Adorno as mentor of Thomas Mann, are: B. Heimann, with his comprehensive essay: *Th, Mann's "Doktor Faustus" und die Musikphilosophie Adornos, Dt. Vis. f. Literaturwiss u Geistesgesch.,* 1964. L. Bergsten, *Op. cit.* Perlini, *Che cosa ha veramente detto Adorno.* Roma, 1971. Idem, *Utopia e prospettiva in Lukacs.* Bari, 1968.

26. "Denn in der Kunst haben wir es mit keinem bloss angenehmen oder nutzlichen Spielwerk, Sondern...mit einer Entfaltung der Wahrheit zu tun", *Theorie Werkausgabe*

(15) 573.

27. Tübingen, 1949.

28. The *Philosophie* was to Mann a more abundant source than ever the accurate work by L. Bergsten shows. In very numerous occasions and places, in the novel, you can find entire propositions which correspond, almost verbatim, to places in the *Philosophie*. We cannot give, here, concrete evidence of the mentioned correspondence. Evidently, we rule out the possibility that Adorno might have echoed Mann. The parallel places are far too clearly characteristic words and concepts of Adorno's philosophy.

29. See my *La filosofia della musica nel pensiero di Th. W. Adorno* . Roma, 1972.

30. For a critical verification of the expressionistic movement, see P. Chiarini, *Caos e geometria*. Firenze, 1969.

31. The word is used for the first time thematically by Lukacs in his *Geschichte und Klassenbewusstsein*. 1923.

32. See *La filosofia della musica*, pp.16-27.

33. See *Dr Faustus,* ch. XXII, pp.184-9.

34. The world of Beethoven is no longer. See Lukacs, op. cit. pp.76-77. E. Heller, *Die Reise der Kunst* ..., 50: The Ninth Symphony is taken back, "because it is no longer truthful". E. Heller, in his "The Ironic German" speaks of the "end of the sonata". Adrian Leverkühn says: *Es darf nicht sein!*. This expression characterises Adorno's entire philosophy.

35. See *La filosofia della musica* ..., 29.

36. *Ibid.*

37. O. Spengler, *Der Untergang des Abendlandes* . München,1922; J. Huizinga, *The Crisis of Civilisation.* 1935. D Cantimori, presenting the Italian edition of Huizinga's work does not hesitate in calling Adorno a *Revenant,* indebted to the author of the *Crisis.*

38. Amsterdam, 1947. New Edition: Frankfurt a.M., 1969.

39. See the Preface to the *Philosophie.*

40. *Dialektik der Aufklärung*, 9ff.

41. The Works of Francis Bacon, *Novum Organum.* Vol. XIV, London, 1825 31; *De augmentis scientiarum*, vol. VIII, 152.

42. See F. O'Farrell, "The Need for Philosophy", *Gregorianum.* 1970, pp.158-9.

43. Not sufficient philosophical attention has been paid, and is being paid, to a thinking consideration of the *technical world*, and of the place that in it should and could occupy art, religion and philosophy. Generally speaking, and particularly in English-speaking philosophical circles, it appears that propositions such as Hegel's *death of art,* Nietzsche's *death of God*, Heidegger's *death of thought,* are light-heartedly met with,

and even more light-heartedly dismissed as gratuitous, poetical pronouncements, deprived of any truth whatsoever.

44. See, *Dialektik der Aufklärung*, "Kulturindustrie", pp.128-76.

45. The *Philosophie der neuen Musik* could be understood as the thematisation of art as denouncement and negation, art as protest. The same character and vocation of art is illustrated by Albert Camus in his *L'homme revoltté* and is, by now, a sort of common recurrent concept to be found, even if only superficially justified, in literature and art criticism.

46. *Prisms. London*, 1967, p.34.

47. *Negative Dialektik,* p.353.

48. A concretely lived illustration of such an experience has been recently given by the confessions of Martin Gray, A Polish jew miraculously escaped from the destruction of Warsaw's ghetto and from Treblinka, the Auschwitz of Poland. His book, *Au nom de tous les miens* (Paris, 1971), a recollection of an absurd journey through a hell of barbarism, is ran through and through by one saddening question: "Why are you not dead? Are you not ashamed of being still alive? Your life is a scandal!" (ch.1).

CHAPTER NINE: STRUCTURALISM, AVANT-GARDE, SEMIOTICS

1. Claude Lévi-Strauss, *The Raw and the Cooked*. London, 1969, pp.1-32. The text of the *Overture* is also to be found in J. Ehrmann, (ed.), *Structuralism*. New York: Anchor Books, 1970, pp.31-55. Part of my argument has been inspired by U.Eco's *La struttura assente*. Milano, 1968 (VII ed.). My analyses are heavily indebted to this outstanding work, in particular. Besides the quoted texts, see also: J.Piaget, *Le Structuralisme*. Paris: P.U.F., 1974 (VI ed.); R.Bastide. (ed.), *Sens et usage du terme structure*. The Hague: Mouton, 1962.

2. P. Bridgam, *La logica della fisica moderna*. Torino, 1965, p.75.

3. Thus Bastide in his *Introduction* to the quoted text.

4. Lévi-Strauss quotes a passage from Pierre Boulez' *Relévés d'apprenti*. Paris, 1966, p.297, which I think worth reporting in a more extensive and meaningful version. "The series embodies a plurivalent mode of thought...It constitutes, therefore, a reaction against traditional musical thought which sees the form as practically pre-existent and as a general morphology. Here [according to serialist thought] there are no pre-construed scales, no general structures into which one may insert or set particular ideas. Quite to the contrary, the composer's thought, operating in accordance with a determined methodology, creates the objects it needs and the form necessary for their organisation, each time he wants to express himself. Classical tonal thought is based on a world defined by gravitation and attraction, serialist thought on a world that is perpetually expanding". In other words, serialist thought and the poetics of avant-garde aim at

producing polysemic and open messages, while questioning any predisposed grammar or code. This, however, does not mean that twelve-tone, serial and post-Webern music, or modern art in general, produce totally amorphous and un-structured phenomena, as Lévi-Strauss would make us believe. For a more detailed discussion and treatment of the poetics and aesthetics of new music, see the preceding chapter. Adorno, quite correctly, understands free-tonal expressionism and serial composition as the attempt to articulate messages against the paralysing practice of schlerotised idioms or codified, reified grammars which had exhausted their communicative and constructive possibilities anyway. Against Lévi-Strauss' specific criticism and against the common perception according to which serial music lacks internal coherence, see Leo Apostel's "Symbolique et anthropologie philosophique: vers une hermeneutique cybernetique", *Cahiers Internationaux du Symbolisme*, Vol.5, 1964, pp.7-31. In this essay, the author offers an eloquent analysis to show that the poetic procedures of serial composition find a perfect isomorphism in the four basic logical operations discussed by J. Piaget in his *Traité de logique*.

5. Once again, I direct the reader to the previous chapter.

6. See Lévi-Strauss, *Eloge de l'anthropologie*. Paris, 1960; *Structural Anthropology*. New York: Anchor Books, 1967, pp.61 and 70; *Overture* to *The Raw and the Cooked*, pp.12-14.

Excellent comments to these selected texts are to be found in: A. Bonomi, "Implicazioni filosofiche nell'antropologia di Claude Lévi-Strauss", *Aut-Aut*, 1967, pp.96-97; U. Eco, *La struttura assente*, pp.288ff. and 312-7. At pages 300-1 of the same book, Eco articulates the most lucid critique of structuralist methodology, as practised by Lévi-Strauss. "If the method is contradictorily understood as the objective logic isomorphous with the universal structural laws, then, obviously, Lévi-Strauss is right in the same way in which the Medieval philologist was right when, faced with contradictions among different texts of the Scriptures, and then between these texts and their interpretations by some *auctoritas*, he would claim that either he had not understood the texts or that there might be some mistake in the transcriptions! Anyway, given the presupposition of a *logica universalis*, there is no room for the real possibility of a contradiction. Indeed, there is no contradiction. However, even this conclusion is correct only if the *Ur-code* (surrendering its universal claims) presents itself as a particular code, a model and a structure, that posits one particular set of ordering laws and excludes all other possible laws".

7. The well known, yet hardly ever clearly and fully explained, incident that occurred between Srafa and Wittgenstein, during a train journey, comes to mind. A gesture (codified in the body language of Italians) of sceptical dismissal, by Srafa, challenged and questioned Wittgenstein's model of language as pictorial of states of affairs and as

isomorphous with the laws of logical discourse.

8. A more extensive, developed and sophisticated conception of harmony is to be found in A. Schöenberg's *Harmonielehre* (Vienna, 1911), which rests on the experimental and revolutionary findings by H. von Helmholz, in his *Die Lehre von den Tonempfindungen*. Leipzig, 1863.

9. I refer the reader to U. Eco's *The Open Work*, a seminal and fundamental text for the understanding of avant-garde poetics and its philosophical implications. In this book, the author analyses, among other works, Stockhausen's *Klavierstück XI*, Berio's *Sequenza per flauto solo*, Pousseur's *Scambi*, Boulez' *Third Sonata for Piano*. The score of *Klavierstück XI* is a large sheet of music paper with a series of note groupings. The performer can choose any of these groupings, to start the piece, organise the sequence and order of succession, elaborate the suggested themes and improvise the connections between the groupings. Obviously, every interpretation/performance will be different. The piece is actually an infinity of possible compositions, performances and interpretation. Berio's *Sequenza* presents a text which predetermines the succession and the intensity of the sounds to be produced. The performer, however, is free to choose the duration of the single notes. For his *Scambi*, Pousseur has written down the following instructions: "*Scambi* is not so much a musical composition as a field of possibilities, an explicit invitation to exercise choice. It is made up of sixteen sections. Each of these can be linked to any two others, without weakening the logical continuity of the musical process. (...) Since the performer can start or finish with any one section, a considerable number of sequential permutations is made available. Furthermore, the two sections which begin on the same theme can be played simultaneously, so as to present a more complex structural polyphony...". Boulez' *Third Sonata for Piano* present a mixture of indeterminacy, freedom of organisation and strictly binding instructions. As a final and extreme example of avant-garde poetics, think of Joyce's *Finnegans Wake*, particularly its circular structure and the endless possibilities of its reading, according to the endless number of possible divisions and connections. In all the mentioned cases, we notice that the performer, the listener or the reader are called to participate in the actual making of the works which can be defined, quite literally, as *unfinished*. The author hands the work to the performer, the listener, the reader, as if the work were a set of components in a construction kit.

10. See U.Eco's *The Aesthetics of Chaosmos. The Middle Ages of James Joyce*. The University of Tulsa, 1982.

11. See U.Eco's *A Theory of Semiotics*. Bloomington: Indiana University Press, 1976, par.1.1.

12. See U.Eco's "The Semantics of Metaphor", in *The Role of the Reader*. Ibidem, 1979. See also Eco's *Lector in fabula*. Milano, 1979.

13. Even for this synthetic summary of the central and distinguishing features of structural thought, on the one hand, and serialist thought, on the other hand, I confess my debt to Eco's pertinent pages in *La struttura assente.*

CHAPTER TEN: DANTE'S *PARADISO* AND THE AESTHETICS OF LIGHT

1. W. Benjamin,. "Die Aufgabe des Uebersetzers", in *Illuminationen,* Schriften, Bd. I. Frankfurt am Main, 1955, pp.40-54.

2. J.L. Borges, "La esfera de Pascal", in *Obras Completas.* Buenos Aires, 1974, p.636.

3. Among the vast literature on this aspect of Medieval culture, see in Particular: R. Assunto, *Die Theorie des Schönen im Mittelalter.* Cologne, 1963; and *Ipotesi e postille sull'estetica medievale, con alcuni relievi su Dante teorizzatore della poesia.* Milano, 1975; E. de Bruyne, *Etudes d'esthétique médiévale.* Bruges, 1946; U. Eco,. *Il problema estetico in Tommaso d'Aquino.* Milano, 1970, and "Sviluppo dell'estetica Medievale", in *Momenti e problemi di storia dell'estetica.* Milano, 1968; W. Tartarkiewicz, *History of Aesthetics,* Vol.1. The Hague, Paris, Warsaw, 1970.

4. In his *Epistola* 13 (61), addressed to Cangrande della Scala, Dante expresses the same thought: *divinum lumen ...penetrat quantum ad essentiam, resplendet quantum ad esse.*

5. This formulation expresses, in minimal terms, the Medieval conception of the cosmos, systematised by Aquinas (see. U. Eco, *op.cit.*) and treasured by Dante.

6. With reference to this epistemological principle and to T. Burckhardt's mentioned observation, we note that the damned in the *Inferno* are equally obsessed with the memory of earthly things.

7. II *Corinthians* 12: 2-4.

8. The harmony of the spheres had been suggested by the Pythagoreans and later by Plato. It seems more likely that Dante knew the version of this idea given by Cicero in his *Somnium Scipionis.*

9. A modern treatment of the same idea is given in G.M. Hopkins' *As Kingfishers Catch Fire.*

10. *Intelletto ed amore* are the essential qualities of *cor gentile.* I would like to note that Guinicelli's poem *Al cor gentil* ..., assumed as the *manifesto* of *Dolce stil novo,* insists much on the metaphorical parallelism obtaining between love, fire and spiritual light.

11. On Grosseteste and his philosophy of light, see James McEvoy's magisterial work: *The Philosophy of Robert Grosseteste.* Oxford, 1982.

12. "Light, therefore, is the beauty and attire of every visible creature. (...) The first word of God created the nature of light. (...) Light is beautiful in itself because its nature is simple and is for itself everything at the same time. Therefore, it is most

uniform and, because of its equality, stands in most harmonious proportion to itself. And the harmony of proportions is beauty. Therefore, regardless of the harmonious proportions of physical shapes, light itself is beautiful and most pleasant to behold".

CHAPTER ELEVEN: FELLINI'S POETICS OF MEMORY

1. It would be true to say that *Amarcord* presents, content-wise at least, ideas, to be found in Fellini's earlier and by now universally recognised masterpieces, the paternity of which must be ascribed to the genial scriptwriter, scenographer and *mentor* Tullio Pinelli not less than to Fellini himself.

2. See R. Bazin: *Qu'est ce que le cinema?* Paris, 1962, p.37.

3. St. Augustine identified the activity of remembering with the experience of *inspectio,* of reading inside oneself. The German verb *erinnern* suggests the same experience of *interiorising*. The Italian *ricordare*, rooted on *cor-cordis*, suggests that to remember means to *bring to one's heart*.

4. "The artist who, free of mental prejudices and of the sterility of the heart, has kept untouched his visual and visionary disposition (talents), penetrates the depths of man's soul...he is, then, carried by as natural *elan*, beyond his limited experience of life and of suffering, beyond himself...Of all natural dynamic forces, art is the most powerful and the most apt to carry the human mind up to the peaks of experience. The aesthetic emotion nourishes a sort of mystical contemplation: it stems out of a religious *humus* on which can fully unfold the spiritual potentialities that lead man, the humble and the powerful, toward the desire and the conquest of truth". Thus Federico Fellini, in his preface to *Panoramique sur le 7me art.* Paris, 1962, pp. 7-8.

5. "The cinema of the aloof, which fed our youth, is definitely turned into the cinema of the absolute vicinity...The film, of which we thought we were only spectators, is in fact the story of our lives. This is the reason why Fellini deeply perturbs us: because he forces us to admit that precisely what we may like to remove far away from us, that is innermost to us". Thus Italo Calvino, in his *Introduction to Fellini. Quattro film.* Torino, 1974.

6. The clown is, sometimes, metamorphosed, into the figure of the magician, the show-man, the hermaphrodite, the medium.

7. At the party the same magician had brought back to Anselmi's memory the magic formula which, as a child, Guido used to utter as an exorcism against the presence of feared ghosts, the formula: *Asa Nlsi MAsa,* the cryptogram for *ANIMA.*

8. It should be remarked how, only with the revolution of modern art at the beginning of this century, the clown, as a central theme and motif, enters the realm of art.

9. For the entire sequence, Zampanò is placed in the middle, between Gelsomina and *il matto.*

10. André Bazin *Qu'est ce que le cinema?*, pp.122-45. The essay on *Cabiria* is now translated in: *What is Cinema?* Vol. 11. The University of California Press, 1971, pp.83-92.

CHAPTER THIRTEEN: THE GAME OF THE NAME THE ROSE PLAYS
1. It is worth remembering that Eco started his academic activities as a Medievalist, publishing, in his early twenties, *Il problema estetico in Tommaso d'Aquino* and, shortly afterwards, the chapter *Sviluppo dell'estetica medievale* for the first volume of *Momenti e problemi di storia dell'estetica,* by Marzorati. The latter has been splendidly translated by Hugh Bredin, with the title: *Art and Beauty in the Middle Ages.* Yale University Press, 1986. These are only two of the major publications, by our author, on Medieval times.
2. The charm of the poem and the relative difficulty the reader may experience in searching for the text, encourage me to produce its first two stanzas:

> Omnis mundi creatura / quasi liber et pictura / nobis est in speculum; / nostrae vitae, nostrae mortis, / nostrae status, nostri sortis / fidele signaculum.
> Nostrum statum pingit rosa, / nostri status decens glosa, / nostrae vitae lectio: / quae dum primo mane floret, / defloratus flos effloret, / vespertino senio.

3. *Opera aperta.* Milano, Bompiani, 1962. *Le poetiche di Joyce* represents a previous contribution to the theory of avant-garde. That work has been reformulated and published in English as *The Aesthetics of Chaosmos.* The University of Tulsa, 1982.
4. I will only mention the abundant use of archaisms, latinisms, barbarisms, quotations, elenchi, praeteritio and a summa of rhetorical devices. With this, perhaps more than with the structure of the novel according to the order of canonical hours, Eco plays his intertextual game with Joyce. I am urged to observe that the highly sophisticated wealth of narrative skills and poetic solutions is craftily concealed by the expert hand of Umberto Eco. Art loves to hide.

CONCLUSION
1. I also refer to Heraclitus, Fr. B 50, where the philosopher announces that the ultimate intelligibility consists in the unification of totality: *En Kai Pan.*
See Martin Heidegger's interpretation of Heraclitus' Fragment, in *Vorträge und Aufsätze.* Pfüllingen, 1954; and in *Was ist das—die Philosophie?* Pfullingen, 1956.
2. "In order to extract from what the words say, what those words want to say, every interpretation must necessarily employ some violence". Martin Heidegger, *Kant und das Problem der Metaphysik.* Bonn, 1929, p.192. See also E. Betti, *Teoria generale della interpretazione.* Milano, 1955 (Cap. III: "Metodologia ermeneutica"); and G. Mounin, *Teoria e storia della traduzione.* Torino, 1965, pp. 13-26.

3. The idea of *constellation*, with its link to the idea of *utopia* and the understanding of philosophical discourse as *fragment*, is convincingly presented in Theodor Wiesengrund Adorno's *Negative Dialektik*. Frankfurt am Main, 1966, (Part II).

4. Plato, *Resp.* X, 596.

5. *Metaph.* 1032b 1; *Nic. Eth.* 1140a 9; Po. 1451b 27; *Ph.* 190a 5. See Chapters five and seven of this text.

6. Instances of these difficulties and unease at defining art and beauty are to be found, among numerous others, in C.K. Ogden and I.A. Richards, *The Meaning of Meaning*. London, 1972, 1923, pp. 139-159; and in a more recent book, rigidly within the analytical tradition and spellbound by the figure of Wittgenstein looming over-large: B.R. Tilghman, *But is it Art?* Oxford, 1984..

7. See Umberto Eco, *Il problema estetico in Tommaso d'Aquino*. Milano, 1970; and Joseph De Finance, *Connaissance de l'être*. Paris-Bruges, 1966, pp. 193-206.

8. Wladislaw Tatarkiewicz, *History of Aesthetics*. The Hague-Warsaw, 1970, Vol. 1, p. 139.

9. See C.R. Rogers, "Towards a Theory of Creativity", *ETC: A Review of General Semantics* 11. 1954, 249-260.

10. See, in particular, H.G. Gadamer, "Die Universalität des hermeneutischen Problems", in *Kleine Schriften*. Tübingen, 1967, Vol. 1, p.106. See also the excellent and inspiring book by Richard Kearney, *Poétique du possible*. Paris, 1984.

11. Gadamer, in his *Wahrheit und Methode*. Tübingen, 1965, speaks of art as "Verwandlung ins Gebilde". This felicitous expression could also be rendered as "metamorphosis into image".

12. See M. Heidegger, "Der Ursprung des Kunstwerkes", in *Holzwege*. Frankfurt, 1952.

13. See U. Eco, *A Theory of Semiotics*. Bloomington, 1979, pp. 22-24; and L. Santoro, *Presupposti filosofici dell'arte moderna*. Urbino, 1978, p.17.

14. See U. Eco, *ibid.*

15. See U. Eco, "Semantique de la metaphore", *Tel Quel* 55. 1973.